BERNARD DUNNE

THE ECSTASY AND THE AGONY

BARRY FLYNN

Contents

INTRODUCTION

When Bernard Dunne left the O2 Arena, bound for
Beaumont Hospital, in the early hours of Sunday 27 September 2009, a thousand bewildering thoughts must have
filled his head. The world title that he had won in emphatic fashion six months previously had become a distant and fading memory. The lights, noise and cruel
drama of the previous evening had left him sore and
shell-shocked as the 'Silent Assassin' from Thailand,
Poonsawat Kratingdaenggym, had deposed, without
mercy, Ireland's boxing king. Losing a world title is a
painful experience; to lose it in such an absolute and
complete fashion is devastating. However, Dunne's career cannot be judged on two minutes of agony in the
white heat of the O2 Arena that night. The journey that
put Dunne at the very top of his profession was long
and arduous. He suffered setbacks that would have
made a lesser fighter walk away from the sport. Most

importantly, he persevered, made his critics eat their words and brought pride to the nation.

Irish sport has given us some fantastic memories over the decades. In 1956, Ronnie Delany's triumph in the 1500 metres at the Melbourne Olympics had cinemas across Ireland packed for days afterwards as newsreels relayed the race to a proud nation. In the recent past, we have enjoyed Ray Houghton's goal in 1988 against England; Packie Bonner's save, followed by David O'Leary's penalty against Romania, at Italia 1990; and indeed Michael Carruth's gold medal in Barcelona in 1992. In each case, the nation rejoiced as one.

In 2009, we got not one but two special sporting moments to savour. In the late afternoon of Saturday 21 March, the Irish rugby team won the grand slam with a heart-stopping 17–15 victory over Wales at the Millennium Stadium in Cardiff. It was the first time that Ireland had achieved such an honour since a Karl Mullen-inspired team achieved similar glory in 1948. The nation rejoiced; but better was to come. That evening, Bernard Dunne produced a performance of sheer class and determination and knocked out Ricardo Cordoba to take the world super-bantamweight title. The determination and commitment shown by Dunne that evening elevated him to the hall of Irish sporting greats, and nothing will ever diminish that performance. He gave us a fight to remember and a reason to feel proud. The glory lasted just six months, until he lost his title to the hard-punching Thai, Poonsawat Kratingdaenggym, in front of nine thousand shocked fans at the O2 Arena. The fact that he rose so high, then fell so far, shows what a cruel sport professional boxing can be.

The story of Bernard Dunne is one of endurance and dedication. As an amateur, he was Ireland's brightest prospect, and suffered the agony of being denied a place at the Sydney Olympics through the lottery that was the qualifying system. He said his goodbyes to the amateur game and took a chance in the United States as a paid fighter. He was highly regarded but still had to fight for everything he achieved in the early part of his paid career. It is hard to appreciate the loneliness and pain that Dunne endured as he learnt the reality of professional boxing in Los Angeles; still he persevered. Injuries, career-threatening brain scans, homesickness and sheer boredom were all sent to try the Dubliner, but he overcame all these obstacles with flying colours. Promoters went bankrupt, others moved on, but Dunne kept his faith and ambition and trained even harder to make it to the top. Eventually, with his apprenticeship finished, he came home to Ireland to follow his dream. Along with Brian Peters and Harry Hawkins, Dunne rejuvenated Irish professional boxing. The sport is, thanks to Dunne, on the crest of a wave, with clubs across the country reporting record levels of membership. Dunne was the hero that everyone wanted to emulate.

In 2009, he achieved his goal as his waist was adorned with the World Boxing Association's super-bantamweight belt; he was the world champion. Eighteen months previously, he had lost his European crown to the clunking fists of the Spaniard Kiko Martinez. Quitting the ring was never going to be an option for Dunne; boxing was his lifeblood, and he knew he had a point to prove. On the road to beating Cordoba, he showed that he had endurance, spirit and, most importantly, the ability to make it back to the top.

In sport, one thing is certain: greatness is forever. If you win an Olympic medal, you are an Olympic medal-winner for the rest of your life; nobody can ever take that achievement from you. The same is true of professional boxing: if you have ever held a world championship belt, you keep that honour with you for the rest of your days. John Caldwell, Steve Collins, Wayne McCullough, Dave 'Boy' McAuley and Barry McGuigan will always be remembered as world champions – men who, regardless of how their careers ended, had reached the very top of their professions. In July 2009, I, along with countless others, attended the funeral of the legendary John Caldwell in his native Belfast. In his prime, John had brought immense pride to his city; he claimed the world bantamweight crown in 1961. He had retired in 1964, but his legacy lived on in the collective memory as a man who, through class, skill and dedication, had reached the very top. Time will never diminish greatness.

Bernard Dunne's achievements in the ring will always be a source of pride to Ireland. This book is a tribute to Bernard and to the people who made his dream a reality. His place in the history books of Irish sport is assured.

He reached the very top of his profession, and nobody will ever take that accomplishment from him. He is, regardless of whether he returns to the boxing ring or not, a legend. An absolute legend.

1

LIKE FATHER, LIKE SON

As the old cock crows, the young cock learns
Irish proverb

Being the son of an exceptional amateur boxer is no bad thing when you are building a career of your own in the sport. For Bernard Dunne, having Brendan Dunne as his father provided him from his earliest days with a ready-made, but playful, sparring partner. The fact that Brendan had represented Ireland at the Montreal Olympic Games was a sure sign that he possessed an excellent boxing pedigree, which his son would inherit. The greatness of the father would, of course, rub off on the son: from no age at all, Bernard was taught how to throw a punch, defend himself, bob, weave, feint, counter-punch and generally hold his own in the Dunne family championships. From the informal lessons of the living room in the early 1980s to the adulation of the adoring crowds in Dublin's O2 Arena in 2009, Brendan Dunne was a constant tower of strength for his son. Being a father, a trainer, a psychologist, an adviser and a shoulder to cry on were all part of the unpaid work that Brendan undertook as Bernard learned his trade in the ring. For Dunne Junior, Dunne Senior was, and is, irreplaceable.

Born in 1954, Brendan Dunne was associated with the Phoenix Boxing Club in Dublin in his formative years. From an early age, he was making his mark in Dublin's National Stadium as one of Ireland's most promising amateur prospects. At the National Juvenile Championships in April 1972, he was awarded the Simon Donnelly Trophy for the most outstanding boxer of that year's tournament. He was fast building a reputation as a skilful light-flyweight and became a regular on the Dublin tournament circuit. In the opening session of the National Junior Championships in January 1973, the *Irish Times* reported that 'the highly-rated Dunne was the most impressive performer of the evening' after he beat Lisburn's Noel Reynolds on his way to taking the title. The following month, Dunne earned a call-up to the Irish under-19 squad for a challenge against the might of England at London's Seymour Hall. Although Ireland lost the match 8–3, Dunne's performance in beating Graham Austin was one of the high points of the night, as he fought with 'great determination' and 'no little skill', according to the *Irish Times*.

In March 1973, aged eighteen, Dunne received his first call-up to the Ireland senior team, for the annual Kuttner Shield clash with Scotland. This international cap was a double honour for Dunne: he became the first boxer ever to represent Ireland in the light-flyweight class, a division which had only been introduced to the Olympic Games in 1968. On the night he was, however, out-boxed by the vastly more experienced Jim Bambrick, who, as reported by the Dublin press the following morning, was 'far too clever' for Dunne and won all three rounds with ease. Despite this defeat, Dunne was maturing fast, and the Irish Amateur Boxing Board showed their faith in him in June of that year by selecting him to represent Ireland in the European Championships in Belgrade. It was again not to be: he was overawed by the Bulgarian Beyhan Fuchedzhiev – the eventual silver medallist – in his opening bout.

Soon, the name Brendan Dunne became a permanent fixture in the light-flyweight berth for Ireland, despite the fact that he was still classed as a junior. It was a steep learning curve for the seventeen-year-old, who was being groomed for the 1976 Olympic Games in Montreal. Further international caps followed, along with a three-fight tour of the United States in late 1973. In March 1974, Brendan won his first Irish senior title – and became the first-ever Irish light-flyweight champion – when he battled his way past the reigning junior champion, Paddy Aspell, at the National Stadium. Dunne's ability to fire quick and effective combinations was pivotal to the victory, while Aspell had proved to be a lot tougher than many observers had anticipated.

Despite not being included in the the Irish team to

compete at the inaugural World Amateur Boxing Championships – held in Cuba that summer – Dunne's status was further enhanced with a victory over Scotland's Martin Lawless in September as the new season opened at the National Stadium. As 1975 dawned, the Irish light-flyweight title again came Dunne's way, and in May that year he impressed in Dublin against England's Joe Dawson. It was an exhilarating display by the Dubliner, and cemented his place in the Irish team bound for that year's European Championships in Katowice in Poland.

The team that travelled to Poland in 1975 had high hopes of equalling Ireland's magnificent three-bronze-medal haul in Madrid in 1971. Davy Larmour from Belfast was the reigning Commonwealth Games champion, while Charlie Nash from Derry had represented Ireland with style at the Munich Olympics in 1972. Along with Brendan Dunne at light-flyweight, the team was made up of Fermanagh's Gordon Ferris at light-heavyweight and Terrence Riordan, from the British Railways Club, at light-middleweight. For Brendan Dunne, the experience of these championships was again to be a bitter one. Yet again, he lost his opening bout, when Poland's Henryk Srednicki stopped him in the first round. For a man hoping for Olympic glory, tournament boxing was proving to be a hard cross to bear. Srednicki was indeed a class act: he would go on to claim the world amateur crown in 1978, as well as appearing in two Olympic Games.

In tournaments, sometimes it boils down to the luck

of the draw. Some boxers can grow in confidence after an opening win, but Brendan Dunne had come across two superb boxers in his opening fights in consecutive European championships: the draws had not been kind to the twenty-year-old Dubliner. As it turned out, the Irish team returned empty-handed from the championships, with Davy Larmour coming closest to a medal, losing to the up-and-coming talent that was England's Charlie Magri at the quarter-final stage.

The 'real deal' as far as every amateur boxer is concerned is the Olympic Games. In Ireland's case, the nation has a proud pedigree at this level, beginning in 1952 in Helsinki, when John McNally won a silver medal in the bantamweight class. Four years later, Ireland took home an astounding total of four medals, with Fred Tiedt taking silver and John Caldwell, Freddie Gilroy and Tony 'Socks' Byrne all taking bronze. But the limelight truly belonged to Ronnie Delany, who claimed gold for Ireland in the 1500 metres on the last day of the Games.

Boxing had provided the country with five Olympic medals in the space of four years, and hopes were high for the Rome Olympics of 1960. However, the Irish team's trip to the Eternal City yielded no medals. Four years later, Belfast's Jim McCourt took a bronze in the lightweight division in Tokyo. With the Montreal Games approaching, McCourt's achievement twelve years previously had been Ireland's last success at Olympic level in any sport. The country was having a barren spell at the highest level, but the squad picked to travel to Canada in

1976 had high hopes of ending the poor run. Brendan Dunne's name was prominent on the list of hopefuls for the games that was submitted to the Irish Olympic Council in February. The other names in the fray included Davy Larmour, Gerry Hamill, Mick Hyland, Brian Byrne and Gordon Ferris. However, Irish boxing has long been renowned for its administrative skulduggery and internal politics; being among the list of 'hopefuls' was no guarantee of success and many tests would be encountered before the final team for Montreal was announced.

In the spring of 1976, Dunne was hitting top form in the National Stadium when he impressed in an international against Germany, where his tall opponent, Bernhard Bülten, received what was in essence a boxing lesson. By the time of the Irish Senior Championships in April 1976, only two men were in contention for the light-flyweight title: Brendan Dunne and Belfast's Jimmy Carson. On the night of the finals, it was Dunne who proved his credentials, booking his ticket to Montreal by winning the title yet again. Joining him on the team were Davy Larmour at flyweight, Gerry Hamill at lightweight, Christy McLoughlin at welterweight and Brian Byrne at light-middleweight. Under Gerry Storey, the team underwent collective training in County Kerry, and on 5 July they left Ireland to fulfil the dream of every sportsman and woman – a trip to the Olympic Games.

The Montreal Olympic Games opened on 17 July 1976; Ireland's best hope of a medal was considered to be the middle-distance runner, Eamonn Coghlan. The boxers got off to the worst possible start when Gerry Hamill was out-pointed in the preliminary round by the Yugoslav, Ace Rusevski. The 4–1 judges' verdict was considered to have been unfair, but the Yugoslav was a decent fighter who went on to claim a bronze medal. For the welterweight Christy McLoughlin, it was to be an equally painful Games: the British star Colin Jones won the contest on a unanimous 5–0 points decision. There was no luck either for Brian Byrne when, after striking lucky and receiving a bye in the draw at the first stage of the light-middleweight class, he lost out to Wilfredo Guzman of Puerto Rico in the second round of competition.

Flying the flag for Ireland, though, was Brendan Dunne, who was victorious over the Japanese fighter Noboru Uchiyama, albeit by a technical knockout. It was an unsatisfactory ending to a fight in which Dunne had built up a slight lead despite being tested by his skilful opponent. During the second round of the bout, in the days of course when headgear was not obligatory, a nasty clash of heads resulted in the Japanese getting a serious gash above his right eye, which prompted the referee to call immediately for the tournament doctor. The blood was gushing from the cut and the officials had no option but to stop the fight and declare Dunne the winner. Despite the manner in which the fight ended, fortune had favoured the Dubliner for the first time in a major tournament. Speaking to Peter Byrne of the *Irish Times* after the fight, Dunne expressed his dissatisfaction at how the contest had ended:

'Naturally, I was not particularly happy with the way that the fight ended, but overall I thought that I did reasonably well. I was caught by a couple of punches in the first round, but on the advice of my cornerman, Gerry Storey, I got my head down in the second and was able to avoid the leather that was coming in.'

In his next bout, Dunne was again to experience the bitter taste of defeat as he came up against the eventual bronze medallist, Orlando Maldonado from Puerto Rico. The fight lasted one round, as Dunne was knocked out. Dunne had again lost to a superior opponent in Maldonado, who would go on to challenge Rafael Orono unsuccessfully for the world super-bantamweight crown in 1983. It was not to be for Brendan Dunne in big tournaments, and he advised the press in the aftermath of the Games that he intended to hang up his vest and try his hand in London as a professional. The most successful Irish boxer at Montreal was Davy Larmour, who was unlucky to lose in the quarter-final to the eventual gold-medal winner, American Leo Randolph, who beat the Cuban Ramón Duvalón in the final. It was a poor Olympics for the Irish boxers – as indeed it had been for Eamonn Coghlan, who finished in fourth place in the 1500 metres final.

The real heroes of the boxing arena at those games were the American boxing team; their biggest star, amongst many, was one Sugar Ray Leonard, who stormed to gold in emphatic style. His professional record would become the envy of every boxer, but even in 1976 he was proving that he had the style, class and charisma to make it to the top. Twenty-five years later, Sugar Ray Leonard and Brendan Dunne would again rub shoulders in the name of boxing as the former world champion signed the son of his fellow former Olympic fighter on professional terms.

Brendan Dunne's promise to turn professional never came to pass. The highlight of his career came at Montreal, and once you have reached such heights, it is hard to climb back to the top. Marriage and family life soon came to overshadow boxing, and on 6 February 1980, the next generation of the international fighting clan was born to Brendan and Angela Dunne in Clondalkin, County Dublin. Bernard Dunne entered a world that was gearing up for the Moscow Olympic Games, which were to be somewhat spoiled by a mass boycott that was instigated in protest of the Soviet Union's invasion of Afghanistan. By August, however, Ireland's medal famine at Olympic level was ended when Hugh Russell claimed a bronze in the flyweight division. The tide was turning for Irish amateur boxing and, twelve years later, at the 1992 Barcelona Olympics, the nation would witness glory in the ring as Michael Carruth struck gold and Wayne McCullough claimed silver.

Like the rest of the populace, sitting watching the glory unfold that morning was a young Bernard Dunne. He had by that stage been bitten by the boxing bug, having followed his two older brothers, Willie and Eddie, into the CIÉ Boxing Club in Inchicore, Dublin in the mid-1980s. Around the time of Bernard Dunne's initiation into the noble art, a legend by the name of Barry McGuigan had captured the hearts of the Irish public with a spectacular display over the then WBA featherweight champion, Eusebio Pedroza. The boxing clubs of Ireland in late 1985 were bursting at the seams in the aftermath of the McGuigan phenomena; the vast majority of those boys never stayed the distance, but Bernard Dunne took a liking to a sport at which he would soon excel. By the age of fifteen, he was knocking out all comers and was seen as a sure bet to emulate his father and go to the Sydney Games. Dunne Junior was a contender who was dedicated to his sport and was collecting Irish schoolboy and junior titles the way that other kids at the time were collecting video games.

In July 1996, Dunne was Ireland's only representative at the Junior Olympic Invitational Event at Marquette, Michigan, in the United States. It was not to be for the Irishman, who lost in the semi-final of the junior flyweight class to the eventual gold medallist, Brian Viloria. However, in attending these games at sixteen years of age, Dunne was progressing perfectly and staking a claim for a place at the Sydney Olympics in 2000. This was Dunne's only goal in boxing, and he had time on his side. Two years later, as Irish senior and junior bantamweight champion, Dunne represented Ireland at the European Championships in Belarus. At a mere eighteen years of age, Bernard had emulated his father in appearing at these games. He had qualified the hard way by fighting both Gabriel Hencz and Myrko Schardein – holders of very impressive records and vastly superior – in order to get to the games. In the championships, he was to lose to the Norwegian Reidar Walstad, whom he would meet again in a professional capacity in 2006. Dunne's teammate, Brian Magee, would go on to win the silver in the middleweight class. However, for both boxers, the Holy Grail of the Sydney Olympics drew nearer, and the real preparations began. Later in 1998, Bernard took the scalp of Canada's Steve Molitor at the National Stadium in Dublin, in what was described by the *Irish Times* as 'an awesome and devastating mix of punching power and polished defensive skills' by the rising Dublin star. Almost a decade later, Molitor would be the IBF superbantamweight champion: Dunne was showing his class.

To say that Bernard Dunne was a promising amateur would be a major understatement. He was untouchable in the Irish bantamweight class and, later that year, at the 1998 World Junior Games in Buenos Aires, he consolidated that reputation within international boxing circles with two excellent wins against Yugoslavia's Zoran Mitrovic and a third-round stoppage of Puerto Rico's Israel Galarza. However, in the quarter-final, Dunne was to lose out on a medal when he was beaten 10–8 by Cuba's Armando Bouza, who would take the silver medal after losing to the classy Hector Perez from Argentina. The Olympic dream was still a reality, though. Closer to home, Dunne was to be tested by Terry Carlyle of the Sacred Heart club in Belfast in the 1999 Irish senior featherweight final and only retained his crown after a count-back was required of the judges' cards. There was disappointment for the rising star later that year when he was eliminated in the opening round of that year's European Championships by Uzbekistan's Tulkunbay Turgunov. Like his father before him, Bernard Dunne had again been unlucky in the opening round of a major games and, with the Sydney Games taking place the following year, it was going to be a tough battle to secure a place through the qualifying competition.

By this stage, Dunne had entered Trinity College Dublin to undertake a course in anatomy. The move to the Trinity also put the bright prospect under the tutelage of the renowned trainer Fred Tiedt, to whom the judges at the 1956 Olympic welterweight final had been – to be kind – less than economical with the pugilistic truth. In boxing terms, he was the victim of a very dubious decision, and in the official report on the 1956 Games he is mentioned as 'probably the most unlucky boxer' to appear at the Melbourne Games. In fact, Tiedt's defeat in 1956 was greeted by a prolonged protest in the arena that threatened to boil over as the judges made their way to safety. A consummate gentleman, Fred Tiedt never got upset about the bad decision and spent the rest of his life – a life that ended prematurely in 1999 – imparting the skills of the game to the up-and-coming boxing talent of Ireland.

In an interview with a college magazine in 2004, Dunne explained how important Trinity had been to his development: 'Boxing opened so many doors for me. Trinity was very different for a person like myself and to this day, it stands to me. I thoroughly enjoyed my time in the college and I still have a lot of friends there. It changed my whole attitude and it was then I knew I wanted to be a professional.'

Already Bernard Dunne's passport was adorned with the stamps of a plethora of destinations as boxing afforded him fantastic opportunities to see the world. Still there was the goal of the Olympic Games to be achieved; qualifying began in earnest in early 2000. The names on everybody's lips as the medal certainties for Ireland were Bernard Dunne and seven-time Irish champion Neil Gough.

In October 1999, Ireland sent a twelve-man squad to the Olympic and European qualifying tournament in Tampere in Finland. Despite the fact that Bernard Dunne impressed, there was no joy for the team. All of these qualifying competitions were costing the IABA large amounts of money, and they were gaining little or no return. The governing body of the sport eventually cut the Irish squad from twelve to ten: Bernard Dunne, Liam Cunningham and Jim Kinsella were the boxers chosen to attend a qualifying tournament in Istanbul in early 2000. Ireland's boxers did not get through the preliminary rounds in Turkey, or at the Chemie Cup qualifying tournament in Germany in March. Despite being fancied to progress, Dunne was eliminated on a disappointing 12–2 score to the Hungarian Janos Nagy in the second round of the competition. The pressure was now on Dunne: the last chance to secure his Olympic place lay at the Tornea Tournament in Venice, three months before the Sydney Olympics were due to commence.

Irish boxing only saw one boxer, Michael Roche from Cork, qualify for the Games; for a country with a fantastic Olympic pedigree in the sport, it was a sad state of affairs. Dunne gave everything in his quest for a place and battled his way through a division with sixty-four entries to face the Finn Joni Turunen in the semi-final. The victor was assured of a place at the Olympics. It was not to be for Dunne, though: the judges gave the Finn the win on a 7–5 decision. Heartbreak was the order of the day for Dunne, who had come so close and yet had still missed out.

There was, however, a small chink of light, in that Dunne had secured the first-reserve spot for the featherweight division and would travel with the Irish team to Sydney. This was not a satisfactory end to a gargantuan effort, but he would travel to Australia anyway – in hope rather than expectation. All he needed was for one boxer to withdraw from the weight division and his dream would be fulfilled. Like a condemned man awaiting news of a reprieve, Dunne waited and waited. There was to be no happy ending, however, as all of those boxers entered in the division weighed-in on time, fit and healthy. Like taking sweets from a child, Irish manager Martin Power had to break the news to Bernard that he would not be competing at the Olympic Games. It was shattering news, and a serious blow to Dunne, who stayed on in Sydney to savour an experience to which he was a mere visitor. There was a good deal of thinking to be done. Amateur boxing had been cruel to Ireland's brightest prospect and, for him, the future was uncertain.

In the end, there was no boxing glory for Ireland at the Sydney Olympics. Michael Roche crashed out on a 17–4 verdict to the Turk Firat Kurugollu in the first round. For Bernard Dunne, the World Amateur Championships in June 2001 was the only prospect on the horizon. Those championships had been secured by Belfast, and the IABA was seeking to send its best possible team to what was a home-based showpiece event. However, the world championships were only a consolation prize in comparison to the Olympic Games. In essence, in amateur sport, the world championships come and go, but being an Olympic champion is a lifelong achievement. Sure enough, the word came out that Bernard Dunne was considering leaving behind his amateur status and turning professional. The IABA, led by its president Dominic O'Rourke, began a process of persuading Dunne to stay in the frame for the 2001 championships. However, after the disappointment of Sydney, the world of amateur boxing had lost its lustre for Bernard Dunne. Frank Warren, the legendary London-based promoter, among others, was interested in securing Dunne's signature for the paid ranks: the race was on to capture the Dubliner. The advisory committee of the IABA pleaded with Dunne to stay with the amateur ranks. They wanted to announce that, in February 2001, a twenty-four-man Irish squad for the Belfast championships would be announced, with Dunne as the shining light of the team. It was not to be. The bitter Olympic experience had changed Bernard Dunne and re-ignited the fighting fire within him; but he would never again compete as an amateur. By early 2001, it was evident that Bernard Dunne had bigger ambitions.

2

CALIFORNIA DREAMING

Work hard, think fast, and you will last
Graffiti in Barry McGuigan's gym, 1981

Despite the pleas from the IABA, and the prospect of future glories, Bernard Dunne's days donning the vest of an amateur were to be consigned to the dustbin of history. In February 2001, Dunne took a leap of faith and made it known that he was going to turn professional; but not until he had made the right move, to the right gym and under the right trainer, promoter and manager. For Dunne, the time to move on had arrived, and there were plenty of big names interested in the precocious Irish talent. He was undoubtedly Ireland's hottest prospect, with 119 victories under his belt in 130 contests as an amateur. The trophy cabinet in the family home was creaking with the weight of his silverware, but that would never provide him with a living. Bernard Dunne was a hungry fighter, and the amateur game had left a bitter taste in his mouth. He wanted to prove himself at the highest levels and was determined to do so. Add to that the fact that he had never been defeated in his own country, and had claimed eleven Irish national titles, and it was evident that Dunne would be a contender in the paid ranks.

However, the step from the relatively clean world of amateur boxing to the dog-eat-dog world of professional boxing is one that cannot be the taken lightly. The world of professional boxing is littered with the ghosts of great amateurs whose talent was never harnessed or allowed to flourish. Too many precocious talents have acquired the tag of 'journeyman' as mismanagement and greed left them washed up and bitter over a sport which promised so much but delivered so little. Ireland has its own fair share of great amateurs (such as the country's first Olympic medallist, John McNally) who could have, and should have, become professional greats only to have become lost in the mire of the paid ranks. The truth is that when money enters the equation in boxing, having class and skill is no guarantee of success. How a boxer is managed becomes absolutely crucial.

However, the most important ingredient in the Bernard Dunne story came in the form of a County Meath man by the name of Brian Peters. The Drumshaughlin publican rejuvenated the world of Irish professional boxing when the game was dying on its feet in this country. In June 1986, Peters had travelled as a fan to Las Vegas to see Barry McGuigan lose his WBA title in stifling heat against the Texan Steve Cruz. That experience ignited within Brian Peters a love of the paid-fight game and all the razzmatazz that went with it. In November 1994, he promoted his first-ever professional bill at the Point Depot in Dublin. Topping the card that evening was Belfast's Las Vegas-based star Wayne McCullough, who defeated Fabrice Benichou over ten rounds. Within seven months, McCullough had taken the WBC bantamweight crown with an epic performance in Japan against the champion Yasuei Yakushiji. The big-time was within Peters's grasp. At the core of Brian Peters Promotions was the fact that Peters was providing Irish professional boxers with a platform on which to parade their skills within their own country. Soon after the Wayne McCullough bill in Dublin, fate was to send the company on to a bigger stage.

In March 1995, Irish boxing enjoyed one of its most successful and memorable evenings. The WBO world super-middleweight fight between Steve Collins and the then reigning champion, Chris Eubank, on St Patrick's weekend, was pure drama from start to finish. The success of the bill, held in Mill Street, County Cork, and co-promoted by Frank Warren and Brain Peters, was due to the fact that Sky Television had transformed the world of boxing and soccer in the early part of the decade. Coverage was 'live and exclusive' all the way, and the super-middleweight scene in Britain and Ireland was flourishing as names such as Eubank and Nigel Benn enjoyed unparalleled exposure on the small screen. In 1993, Belfast's Ray Close fought Eubank in a bloodthirsty encounter at the Kelvin Hall in Glasgow, only to lose to a narrow decision by the judges. However, Close had won the fight in the hearts of the crowd and another crack at Eubank's title was assured. The rematch at the King's Hall in Belfast a year later was again an action-packed encounter, which Eubank shaded by a split decision. The scene was now set for a third contest between Close and Eubank in March 1995. However, a brain scan on Close showed up some 'irregularities' and he was prevented from boxing by the British Boxing Board of Control. At this stage, it fell to Brian Peters to rescue the day: Steve Collins was drafted in to fill the vacancy. Collins's victory that night was the start of a very successful run for Brian Peters Promotions. The rest, as they say, is history.

As Brian Peters Promotions became a force to be reckoned with on the Irish boxing scene, it was inevitable that Bernard Dunne would come under the watchful eye of Brian Peters. By 2000, Peters was convinced that Dunne was boxing dynamite. How he handled the young Irish star was going to be crucial; a hard education in the paid game would give Dunne the edge he needed. Dunne and Peters set their sights on the United States – specifically Los Angeles. They sounded out all the main players in the American fight game. Nobody was considered too big to approach as Peters knew that Dunne was what the Americans call the 'real deal' in paid boxing terms.

Bob Arum was 'Mr Boxing' in Las Vegas. The promoter has an impeccable record in the professional game, having handled names such as Marvin Hagler, Sugar Ray

Leonard and Evander Holyfield. He was impressed with Dunne and made moves towards signing him. So too did Shelly Finkel, who had been involved in overseeing the epic career of the former world junior-middleweight champion Mike McCallum – a legend who had won each of his six title defences by knock-out. Offers were made, and it was a case of weighing up the options and making an informed decision. In the end, Dunne opted for Mat Tinley and Bob Goosen, who oversaw a major boxing promotion company known as America Presents. These people meant business: their list of clients included Mike Tyson, Cuba's Joel Casamayor and, notably, Belfast's own Wayne McCullough.

Freddie Roach was given the task of conditioning Dunne. Born in South Boston, the so-called spiritual home of the Irish in America, Roach had a keen eye for boxing talent. In the mid-1980s, Roach, known affectionately as 'La Cucaracha' – the Cockroach – had definitely been a contender in the featherweight division, having won thirty-nine of his fifty-three fights. He had been a prospective challenger for Barry McGuigan's WBA title, but injury ended his career before he could fulfil his early promise. Undeterred, he established the Wild Card Gym in Los Angeles, where his list of clients has been impressive. Famously, Roach oversaw the career of the actor Mickey Rourke when he took a break from the big screen to try his hand at professional boxing. Roach had strong Irish connections: he had looked after Steve Collins for six of his seven world title defences and had also trained

Wayne McCullough. (Steve Collins once described him as 'more like a Dubliner' in personality than many from the actual city.) In early November 2001, Dunne left Ireland for Los Angeles.

With the right team in place, Dunne outlined his aims and objectives for his fledgling career. The plan was to establish his name within the featherweight class and, with luck, claim the North American Boxing Federation title within two years. Such an accolade would place the Dubliner in the top ten in the world rankings and act as a springboard for him to achieve his ultimate dream of winning of a world title a reality. Speaking to the press when his first American contest was announced, Dunne displayed a confidence, maturity and single-mindedness unusual in one so young:

'I have a three-year plan and I have taken my time picking my team and they have all dealt with top boxers. I'm twenty-one now – I'm a baby. I made a decision in February and spoke to all the promoters. They all offered deals, but this is my best option. If you want to be the best, you have to go to the States, where all the best boxers come from. My father boxed in the 1976 Olympic Games; I've been boxing since I was five and there is nothing else I ever wanted to do.'

Bernard Dunne made the next major step in achieving his dream on 19 December 2001, when he stepped through the ropes at the Feather Falls Casino in Oroville, California, to face the Mexican Rodrigo Ortiz. With a record of three defeats in his first three fights, Ortiz was considered to be the perfect opponent for Dunne to face on his debut. In essence, Ortiz was out of his depth against an eager debutant wanting to establish himself in the paid ranks. In boxing terms, he was a 'chopping block'. There was no dry ice, no 'Irish Rover', no emotional anthems, and no adoring, patriotic crowd to greet Dunne as he made his way to the ring that evening. This was professional boxing at its purest: there was a job to be done, and all the razzamatazz could wait.

In the end, the fight lasted only two rounds. The first round saw Dunne take his man apart in emphatic fashion, with an all-action onslaught. Any nerves he carried with him were soon lost as flurry after flurry of punches landed on the hapless Ortiz. It was a mismatch: Dunne played with his opponent, and the Mexican went to his corner at the end of the first round with a broken spirit – and a broken nose to show for his troubles. It was to be a good night, as the crowd in the 1,200-seat arena warmed to Dunne in the limited time he had in which to show his class. The papers in the States the following day described the debut as 'sensational' and a 'demolition job', but Dunne and his entourage knew that there was a long way to go. Speaking after the bout, Freddie Roach was forthright in his praise of Dunne:

'The kid delivered big time. Bernard also produced some big hits on Ortiz. Mexicans are a durable bunch and guys like Ortiz are learning their trade. It was only his third fight, but he couldn't handle Bernard's big shots.'

With Christmas on the horizon, a trip back home to

Ireland saw Bernard keeping trim at the renowned Holy Trinity Club in Belfast, where, significantly, he was once again to come under the tutelage of trainer Harry Hawkins – a pairing that would ultimately end in glory. The name Hawkins is almost legendary in the Irish fight game, and Harry Hawkins knew Bernard Dunne well. Hawkins had first looked after Dunne when he took charge of an Irish under-17 squad that had toured in Belarus in 1997 – and had been impressed by what he saw. His aim was to prepare Dunne for a second fight, which would take place on 12 January at Cox's Pavilion in Las Vegas. Also on that bill would be Dunne's hero, Wayne McCullough. To share a billing with the former world champion would be a bonus for Dunne as he started out on his own career. However, Dunne's date on the undercard of the McCullough bill fell through at the very end, when a suitable opponent could not be found. This was to become an occupational hazard for Dunne over the years, with numerous opponents failing to keep a date with the Dubliner. For Dunne, it was a case of knuckling down at the Wild Card Gym. It may have been glamourous to take early-morning jogs along Santa Monica beach and live life among the stars of Hollywood, but the road to success would entail many hours of sweat and pain in Freddie Roach's gymnasium. Dunne was still a novice, and the hard work had to be done.

It was to prove to be a long and lonely road, as killing time became the order of the day. Bernard Dunne had to wait until 2 August – a full eight months – before he made his second appearance in the paid ranks, at the Fox-woods Resort in Connecticut. Topping the bill that evening was the clash between Richard La Montague and Michael Bennett for the American IBA super-cruiser-weight title. Dunne's opponent, however, represented the depressing underbelly of professional boxing. Christian Cabrera from the Dominican Republic, who had no amateur record of note, was coming up against one of the most exciting additions to the featherweight scene. Not surprisingly, the fight was over within four minutes, as Dunne again pummelled his opponent. Cabrera was completely out of his depth, and retired from the the sport that night. It was all too easy: Dunne would not learn anything from such charades. Patience was the name of the game for Peters, Roach and Dunne. In boxing, however, you can never tell what trial or tribulation might await you around the next corner. Dunne was to be tested severely, but not within the ropes.

3

TRIALS AND TRIBULATIONS

If you can meet with Triumph and Disaster
And treat those two impostors just the same . . .
'If', Rudyard Kipling

In March 2002, the America Presents organisation announced that it was on the verge of collapse. Faced with
crippling debts, the company left many boxers, including
Bernard Dunne, high and dry. Into the mix came Sugar
Ray Leonard, who, in his first venture into the promotional business, was recruiting raw talent and building a
stable of his own. Leonard had rubbed shoulders with
Brendan Dunne in Montreal in 1976. He had heard good
reports of Bernard 'Ben' Dunne and liked what he saw
in the clips of the Irishman. Leonard put his faith in
Dunne and immediately signed up the talented Dubliner.
He was convinced that 'Ben Dunne' – the Americans
could never get their tongue around the name 'Bernard',
and he was known as plain 'Ben', not of course to be
confused with the Irish businessman Ben Dunne – could

go all the way, and was prepared to spend good money to see him progress. This was a godsend for Dunne. With two wins under his belt and a long-term and potentially very lucrative contract with Sugar Ray Leonard, the world was Bernard's proverbial oyster. His third fight – and his first under Leonard – was due to take place against the Denver-based Mexican Tony Espinosa in Buffalo, New York State, on 18 October, where he would be on the undercard of the Joe Mesi v. David Izon all-American heavyweight grudge match. It was Dunne's big chance to establish his name at an event for which eighteen thousand tickets had already been sold and which was to be televised coast-to-coast in the United States.

As the hurdle of the loss of America Presents was cleared by Dunne, a further, more daunting, obstacle appeared. It is said that adversity builds character in sportsmen and women, and any journey to the top of an individual's sport is rarely without drama, tears and serious doubt: Bernard Dunne's climb up the ranks was to be no exception. In October 2002, Dunne's career was brought to a life-shattering halt as the worst possible news on his health was relayed to him. As the preparations for the fight on 18 October continued, the twenty-two-year-old was told that an 'abnormality' had shown up in a standard brain scan. The fight was off, and Dunne's career – perhaps even his life – was in jeopardy.

Dunne was now facing the biggest fight of his career. The news came at the worst possible time: just twenty-four hours before he was due to enter the ring. The pre-fight weigh-ins and press conferences were taking place at the Holiday Inn in Buffalo when chief matchmaker Ray Katz was told that Dunne had been suspended by the New York State Boxing Commission pending further investigation. On the other end of the phone had been eminent neurologist Dr Barry Jordan, who explained to Katz that there had been a 'problem' following a standard, compulsory brain scan. The abnormality was described as consisting of some 'white matter', but the doubts had been cast on Dunne's future and, as per the rules, he was suspended from the ring until further tests could be carried out.

Within the hall, Katz was not amused. A lot of money was at stake, but all bets were now off. Many fans had booked to see Dunne in action and had travelled from Boston and New York, as well as a few from Dublin, to see their hero. Sugar Ray Leonard's team began to seek answers from the officials in the room, but, in the arena, Dunne was blissfully unaware that the commotion in the room concerned him: he thought that a problem had been identified with his opponent. Eventually, the news was broken to the stunned fighter, and a press conference was hastily arranged to advise the assembled media of the 'difficulties'. It fell to Ralph Petrillo, New York State's chief medical co-coordinator, to break the news to the assembled press that Dunne had been suspended from boxing. At the top of the packed room, Dunne sat dumbfounded as Petrillo stared at him and spoke the words that still haunt the Dubliner to the press:

'Something showed up on the scan: white matter. It's not definitive, and new scans will need to be taken. Due to this, we won't let him fight on the card tomorrow night. But it doesn't rule out his boxing career. I want to see this kid when he's eighty years old and he has children and grandchildren. When you have any potential risk with the brain, among the things that can happen are paralysis, permanent seizures and, in the worst case, you could be killed. We must not allow that.'

Bernard Dunne's career lay in tatters. His dream of a world title was irrelevant: whether he ever even donned boxing gloves again was now in the hands of the medical profession. Dunne was now to endure a nightmare of self-doubt. There is no doubt that boxing is a cruel sport, both physically and emotionally. Many former boxers will admit that the most important aspect of the game is knowing when to retire from the ring before permanent damage is sustained – and there are, unfortunately, plenty of pitiful examples of boxers who stayed in the game for far too long.

In the 1980s, boxing came under immense pressure as many high-profile deaths added to the arguments surrounding the safety of the sport. In 1980, Johnny Owen from Wales fought the fight of his life against Mexico's Lupe Pintor for the WBC world lightweight crown. In the twelfth round, Owen was knocked to the canvas and never regained consciousness: he died two months later. In June 1982, Barry McGuigan took a further step along the road to the featherweight crown when he faced a

Nigerian novice by the name of Young Ali. In the sixth round of their bout, McGuigan secured a knockout of his opponent. Ali was taken to hospital, where he died five months later. McGuigan had to endure his own crisis of confidence in the aftermath of that tragedy, and he almost retired from the sport. Sadly, throughout history, there have been too many cases like those of Johnny Owen and Young Ali.

Boxing today is one of the most heavily regulated sports in the world. The reasons why all fighters must undergo MRI scans are well-documented. Deaths within the ring have over the years scarred the name of the sport. That the aim of a contest is to hit an opponent to the head and body leaves boxing open to claims that it is a cruel sport; indeed, there is always the danger that a blow to the head will inflict death through haemorrhage. There are two schools of thought as to how, given the dangers involved, boxing should be managed. One school adopts a zero-tolerance approach, arguing that boxing should be banned completely. The other argues that boxing can be managed through proper medical and professional advice, as well as regulations. As part of this management, a boxer for whom any problem shows up on an MRI scan must stop boxing until the situation has been clarified. Dunne had no choice but to abide by the professional advice given to the New York Boxing Commission.

It was now a case of managing a career-threatening situation with skill and making sure that the problems highlighted by the scan were clarified. Brian Peters and Sugar Ray Leonard's right-hand man, Bjorn Rebney, advised the Commission that Dunne would undergo further independent tests to establish whether there was a way to resolve the health concerns in time for the fight. However, in the end he was to be a frustrated spectator as time ran out and the fight was cancelled. Sugar Ray Leonard was supportive of his man and felt that he had the character to come through his personal test:

'He has handled it so well, he's so positive, and I'm sure this is only a bump in the road. This has reminded me of when I suffered a detached retina in the build-up to a world title defence against Roger Stafford – scheduled for Buffalo too. I was forced into retirement but I came back to beat Marvin Hagler, and Bernard will come back from this and be stronger.'

Irish boxing has a number of recent examples of boxers whose careers have been adversely affected by similar problems to the one encountered by Dunne. In 1999, Steve Collins, another son of Dublin, was forced to give up the boxing game on the advice of doctors. The offer of a fight with Joe Calzaghe in Cardiff was just the chance that Collins needed to re-launch his career, two years after he had hung up his gloves. However, while sparring with British middleweight champion Howard Eastman in preparation for the fight, he blacked out. He was immediately ordered to undergo a brain scan and was the told by doctors that he had to retire from boxing, this time for good.

There was, of course, another Irish boxer who had struggled long and hard to salvage a promising career after 'irregularities' were discovered in a brain scan. As luck would have it, Wayne McCullough was living in Las Vegas and was on hand to advise Dunne as to how he could address the situation. McCullough had been a boyhood hero of Dunne's and an inspiration to him throughout his amateur career. The 'Pocket Rocket' had, like Dunne, gone to the United States in search of boxing fame and glory. In June 1995, McCullough had defeated the reigning world champion Yashuei Yakushiji, in the fighter's home country of Japan, to claim the WBC bantamweight crown. Later that year, Dunne, as a fifteen-year-old lad, had sparred with McCullough at the gym at Luttrellstown Castle – and had become convinced that Wayne McCullough was the man to emulate.

The irregularities were discovered during a routine annual brain scan carried out at Belfast's Royal Victoria Hospital in October 2000. Two days before he was due to climb into the ring for a comeback bout against the Hungarian Sandor Koszics, McCullough was told that a cyst had been discovered in his brain and that he had been suspended by the British Boxing Board of Control. In essence, he was advised that he could be killed if he continued to box. McCullough, in his 2005 autobiography *Don't Quit*, recalled what a devastating blow the news was to him:

'That was the lowest point in my career. My wife and I could only sit about the house, and I became very depressed. But if anything, I am a fighter, and it was a case of trying to establish the extent of the problem and making sure it was addressed.'

For McCullough, the road to getting back into boxing lay in getting a second opinion: he was directed to specialists in neurosurgery at the University of California in Los Angeles. After further tests, McCullough was advised that the cyst was not in his brain but in the lining between the brain and the skull. While this was an unsatisfactory state of affairs, the finding enabled McCullough to win back his licence in Nevada; and he was eventually cleared to fight in Britain. If anyone could advise Dunne on how to clear his name, it was McCullough.

In the early days after Bernard Dunne moved to Los Angeles, McCullough had been on the end of the phone to offer him advice on his career and, more importantly, on how to beat homesickness. When the news of Bernard's brain scan broke, McCullough told him not to panic. Thinking back to his own experiences, he suggested that Dunne get a second opinion at UCLA. The staff at UCLA had to carry out a series of exhaustive tests before they could begin to make sense of the original brain scan. Charts were studied, and scans were assessed; in the interim, Dunne had gone back to Ireland for a break. By mid-November, six weeks after Dunne's suspension, the neurologists at UCLA had given him the all-clear. Their opinion was that the 'white matter' was, in essence, a normal, and not dangerous, phenomenon that should not deny Dunne the chance to box. However, the ultimate decision lay with the New York Boxing Commission; they were not due to meet until just before Christmas. It was going to be an agonising wait.

For Dunne, the key to coming through this trial of nerves was to remain positive. A fight had been provisionally arranged for him at the Wild West Casino in Oklahoma on 3 January 2003. His opponent, Simon Ramirez, had a record of four fights: two wins, one loss and one defeat. For Dunne, a man facing into the boxing wilderness, the date with Ramirez was a make-or-break fight. But first, he needed clearance to box again. To escape from the pressure, Dunne took himself to the cinema in Dublin on the day when the results of his latest scan were due. The film he went to see was *The Two Towers*, the second instalment of the Lord of the Rings trilogy. Hoping not to disturb anyone, he set his mobile phone to 'vibrate'. He was just settling into his seat to enjoy the movie when the phone lit up and began to vibrate: it was Brian Peters. Holding the phone to his ear, Dunne was given the news he had been waiting for: he had been given the all-clear. What those present in the cinema made of the man who suddenly leapt to his feet and shouted out gleefully during the film was never recorded. The first person to whom Dunne relayed the news was his father Brendan. There were major celebrations in the Dunne household in December 2002: Christmas had come a week early.

The decision to give Bernard the all-clear was made by Barry Jordan, the New York commission's chief medical advisor – who had also been responsible for suspending Dunne in October. Dunne was free to box on 3 January, and Sugar Ray Leonard went back to plotting Dunne's rise up the ladder. All in all, Dunne had been out of action for five months – a gap which could have a serious impact on him, both physically and mentally. The best way to get over the trauma of the brain 'irregularities' was to get straight back into the ring. Leonard spoke to the media as soon as his man had been given the good news:

'I'm thrilled for Bernard on two fronts. Firstly, the tests have established he can come back in perfect physical health, and second, he can resume his career and climb towards the world featherweight title.'

They say that in life you never get a second chance to make a first impression. Bernard Dunne was lucky. He knew that he had been blessed, and now it was up to him not to waste his second opportunity. After he had come so close to having it all taken away from him, Dunne was now determined to make the most of his opportunities: 'I've had a taste now of not being able to do it, and I didn't like it at all, and if anything, I'll be more focused now, more determined to get to the top.'

The comeback fight was now the most important fight of Bernard Dunne's career. Luckily, he had been kept in prime condition by Harry Hawkins in Ireland, and after Christmas Dunne left Dublin to take up from where he had left off. Ramirez was a nineteen-year-old rookie professional from Oklahoma; he had been stopped in two rounds in his last bout, against fellow rookie Cornelius Lock. Ranked 374th in the world, he was the type of opponent that Dunne needed to boost his confidence after the setbacks he had endured. The fight would be broadcast live on ESPN television – giving Dunne the exposure he needed to show the boxing fraternity that he had not been affected by his ordeal and was hungrier than ever. The year 2002 had been a poor one for Bernard Dunne. As 2003 dawned, he knew he had a lot of work to do.

4

Back on the Road Again

You will never plough a field by turning it over in your head.

Irish proverb

Muhammad Ali once said that the two most important things that someone needs to become a star are the 'connections and the complexion'. As he knuckled down for his next fight, Bernard Dunne had both of these attributes in abundance. With the career of Ireland's brightest prospect back on track, the New Year festivities for 2003 were rather subdued for Dunne: he had a date with Simon Ramirez to keep on 3 January. For Dunne, Peters and Leonard, there was now a need to catch up on lost time: two further bouts had been arranged for Dunne within eight weeks of his return to the ring. For the plan to succeed, Dunne would have to play his part by winning, and winning well. Training had gone well back in Freddie Roach's gymnasium and, as the fight approached, Dunne was anxious to return to his winning ways: 'The sparring I get is tremendous, with some of the best fighters in the world, and it's good to be able to hold your own with these guys, it gives you confidence.'

In the end, extra confidence was not needed as Dunne did the job in emphatic fashion. The rookie Ramirez was shown up to be just that – a rookie. After Dunne delivered two of the sweetest left hooks to the body of Ramirez, the man nicknamed 'Too Sweet' doubled over in pain. The referee intervened, and the fight was over after just sixty-nine seconds. Nobody in the Dunne camp was too upset at the mismatch: Bernard was back, and still eager and hungry. Also watching Bernard's victory, on coast-to-coast television across the United States, were an estimated 90 million viewers. The scheduled four-round contest gave Dunne a taste of competition, but the calibre of his opponent was not going to raise any eyebrows in the featherweight division. Still, Sugar Ray Leonard, the commentators and the pundits continued to hail Bernard as the new Barry McGuigan. While the hype was unhelpful, Bernard had a team of professionals around him that were only too keen to keep his feet fixed firmly to the ground. However, the weight of expectation was growing – as was the name and reputation of Bernard Dunne. After the victory, Brian Peters summed up the relief that Dunne had experienced on his return to the ring: 'After the frustration of the last three months, he was in the mood to take it out on someone, and sadly for Ramirez, it was on him.'

Having exorcised the past eleven weeks of annoyance

and pain, Dunne was definitely out to make up on lost time. His next fight was scheduled for 7 February in Las Vegas, where Eric Trujillo – another untried boxer making his debut – was to be the next opponent for the Dubliner. While Dunne's career needed some momentum, his management choose to exercise caution in his choice of opponents. He would have to content himself with rookies and journeymen for the time being. As the saying goes: you can only box what's put in front of you.

Las Vegas, Nevada, is the place to be if you want to make an impression in big-time boxing circles. For Sugar Ray Leonard, Vegas held fond memories from his own sparkling career. In September 1981, one of the greatest fights of all time took place between Leonard and Thomas Hearns at Caesar's Palace for the undisputed world welterweight crown. The fight was pure exhilaration from start to finish: Leonard triumphed in the fourteenth round by knocking out his legendary rival. Six years later, Leonard made a triumphant return to the sport at the same venue and defeated 'Marvellous' Marvin Hagler by a split decision to claim the WBC middleweight crown. Now, Dunne was stepping up to the plate, at the Sam's Town Hotel Casino. It was where he wanted to be – and where Leonard wanted him to make his mark.

Despite the occasion, Dunne was yet again a mere bit player on a seven-card bill that was headlined by the up-and-coming middleweight David Estrada. Although Dunne's fight was scheduled for just four rounds, it was reported that this would be his last outing over such a limited distance. The limelight and the big time must have seemed a million miles away for Dunne as he entered the ring that night to a ripple of applause – and a few bois-terous Irish cheers – in a half-empty arena. All that mat-tered, though, was the result: it was a case of one fight at a time. Despite his status as a novice, twenty-year-old Eric Trujillo had an amateur record of note, having claimed two Golden Gloves titles in his native Colorado. However, Trujillo had no answer to Dunne's class, skill and speed, and he was easy prey for the Neilstown man.

Within seconds of the first bell, Dunne had put his man on the canvas with a sharp right hand. The debu-tant regained his composure and attacked Dunne, hitting him with his own crisp right hook. However, Dunne moved up a gear and again floored his opponent with a stinging left hand to the body. Seconds later, Trujillo's legs had turned to rubber, and after Dunne had admin-istered a double right hand to his opponent which left him prostrate in the ring, it was left to the referee, Tony Weeks, to stop the fight. Game, set and match to Dunne: fought four, won four – all by knockout. For Trujillo, all he had to show from the fight was an aching face and a ban from the ring for a month due to his inability to defend himself competently.

Dunne had still not been tested in his paid career to date. Manager Brian Peters was upbeat on his protégé's progress, however, and indicated that more testing op-ponents lay ahead for Dunne: 'Bernard was exceptional

Dunne with a record of two wins in sixteen contests; despite the defeats, he was relatively experienced compared to Dunne's previous opponents. In the end, the fight went the distance – albeit just four rounds. Within seconds of the opening bell, Dunne had Villa on the seat of his pants as a neat combination caught him cleanly. However, Villa, to his credit, climbed off the floor to mix it with the Dubliner for the rest of the bout. The judges were unanimous in their scoring and gave Dunne all four rounds, by 40 points to Villa's 35. At ringside, Schwarzenegger had been impressed by the Irishman's performance and suggested to reporters that Dunne would become the next Oscar De La Hoya. To be compared to De La Hoya was an unbelievable accolade for Dunne, given that the Mexican was an absolute legend who had claimed a gold medal in the lightweight division at the Barcelona Olympic Games and who had won world titles at five different weights. Indeed, Dunne was to receive a personal invitation from the former Mr Universe to box on the same bill in 2004. Brian Peters, however, knew that continuing to put Dunne into the ring with boxers of the calibre of Villa was doing little to advance his man's career: he was trying to secure a six-round contest in Los Angeles on St Patrick's Day. Dunne needed to be 'stretched' in the ring, and Peters and Leonard were keen to see him go up against a durable opponent. Time was on Dunne's side, though: the TV executives in the United States were keen to track his progress, and his name – and loyal following – was growing by the day.

In the event, the proposed St Patrick's Day fight in Los Angeles did not go ahead, as a suitable opponent could not be found in time. The focus shifted to securing a fight for him at a Sugar Ray Leonard-promoted bill at the Wild West Casino in Oklahoma on 25 April. In the end, twenty-year-old Oscar Rosales from Texas was the man chosen to face Ireland's hottest prospect, over six rounds. Like Dunne, Rosales had five fights under his belt – with two wins, two losses and one draw to his name. He was out of his depth against Dunne, however. The Irish contingent was not to be let down on the evening: Dunne was in sparkling form for the short time the contest lasted. With the bell to end the first round about to sound, Dunne unleashed a vicious combination that left Rosales sprawling – and the referee wisely stepped in to stop the fight. In the *Belfast Telegraph*, correspondent David Kelly described Dunne's performance as 'stunning', while Leonard, the promoter, said that 'this was his first six-rounder and he passed it with flying colours'. Dunne's record now stood at six wins in six bouts, with all but one coming by knockout in either the first or second round. He still to be tested properly; the kid gloves were still on.

The Dunne bandwagon was on a roll. Fight number seven followed on 6 June, against Terrell Hargrove from Louisville, Kentucky. The bill was again to be screened live across the United States; the exposure was helping to establish Bernard as one of the most promising prospects in the featherweight division. For Dunne, the

fight was almost a home appearance, with the bill scheduled for the Mohegan Sun Casino in Connecticut, an
hour's drive from Boston. With large Irish support anticipated, it seemed that Hargrove, with a record of six
wins in eleven contests (he had been stopped only once),
could give Dunne a hard fight. Notably, Hargrove possessed a degree of durability, having been tested over ten
rounds, and also possessed a decent punch: three of his
victories had ended in knockouts. There was no doubt
that this was, on paper, the biggest test that Dunne had
faced in his paid career. It was a gamble that Peters and
Leonard were prepared to take: they had unflinching faith
in Bernard Dunne's class and maturity. He did not let
them down, making light work of Hargrove as flurry
after flurry of punches was followed by sweet right
hooks throughout the opening round. It was a truly awesome display, and the referee had to intervene to save the
hapless Louisville fighter from further punishment. Hargrove was stopped in the first round, and the Irish
contingent was cock-a-hoop.

Although the fight was once again a mismatch, it was
a mismatch with a difference. Hargrove had come to the
ring with a better record than any of Dunne's previous
opponents and yet had suffered the same fate. Dunne
had proved that he had both the talent and the confidence to thrive against such opponents. In the post-fight
interviews, Sugar Ray Leonard had high priase for his
fighter:

'We expected him to beat Hargrove, a decent club

professional who was an excellent test for an up-and-coming fighter. But nobody, not even me, expected Bernard to take him out like that in the first round. It was an awesome display, absolutely stunning. He just went through the guy and made me think: Hang on, just how good is this kid going to be? Ben has it in him to make a very big name for himself in this sport.'

When somebody of the calibre of Sugar Ray Leonard says that about a boxer, people begin to take notice. As an Olympic gold medallist and five-time world champion, Leonard's knowledge of boxing was almost infallible. Dunne had been blessed by one of the game's gods: it was a case of onwards and upwards. It had been a hard few months for Dunne. His management team had kept him active, with a plentiful supply of opponents, and he had passed each test with flying colours. As high summer approached, Dunne was keen to get a break from the daily grind of training and fighting and take a trip back home to Ireland to see his family.

Before he could go home, one more opponent was waiting: Dunne was to make his debut on the American boxing feature *The New Generation*, part of the sports television programme *ShoBox*. The feature was a great place for Dunne to showcase his worth: it had an estimated 19 million viewers. The show prided itself on excellent matchmaking between fighters tipped for future glory. In fact, fighters who have made it to the top after appearing on the show are known as '*ShoBox* fighters'. The programme's producer, Jay Larkin, had been keen to get

Dunne on the show; when Brian Peters received the call from Larkin, the offer was too good to turn down: 'Jay called and he was very keen to have Bernard on the card, but he wanted him to box over eight rounds, which I wasn't keen on at first, but for the sake of a couple of rounds this was too good an opportunity to miss.'

The day of reckoning was to be the eve of Independence Day, 3 July, against another young talent by the name of Mario Lacey, who had a growing reputation and was keen to make a name for himself by getting Dunne's scalp. Lacey had no fewer than five Golden Gloves titles to his name, and there was no doubting that he was rated highly. He had lost only once in eleven professional fights and, in his previous outing, had knocked out Louisiana's John Monroe in Mississippi. He was durable, and could throw an effective punch. Dunne had to be wary and rely on his undoubted talents to overcome Lacey, but this was the perfect opportunity for him to round off an incredible six months since his return to the ring.

The Dubliner's preparations for the fight, in Freddie Roach's gym, were arduous. Hundreds of rounds were sparred, and no stone was left unturned, as the fight approached. Sugar Ray's promoter, Ray Kazt, outlined the progress that Dunne had made to date, and what he should be aiming for in the future:

'The idea is to keep him busy, to progress the level of his opponents, and if he continues to perform the way he has, within a year to eighteen months he can be among the elite featherweights in the world. He's still a young kid and needs to get some rounds in, but he gets unbelievable sparring with guys like Shane Mosley and Manny Pacquiao, which is very good experience for him. He brings a lot of charisma to the ring, he can punch, and he's very fast. When you have all those ingredients, you can be a star.'

The expectations in the arena at the Mountaineer Race Track in Connecticut were for a truly cracking fight, with two well-primed boxers out to make their mark, on live television. Both men had amateur records of note and both knew that defeat at this stage of their career would be a severe setback for them. The Irish contingent from Boston had again travelled in force to cheer on their hero, and the pressure was on Dunne to win, and win well. In the heat of the summer night, referee Tim Wheeler sent the boxers to their corners to await the first bell.

The fight lasted just 111 seconds. Dunne was a sensation in the ring and cut fast and loose, with rapid fists, jabs, hooks and accurate combinations. For the short time the two men were in the ring, he completely overwhelmed Lacey: he was knocked to the canvas twice by sharp left hooks and sent to his corner a beaten man. The Dunne contingent was gobsmacked by the display. The script could not have been written any better: Dunne had proved that he was made for big-time television. He had it all: speed, aggression, an ability to punch and, most importantly, absolutely no fear. As he left the arena that night, he was walking on air.

Speaking after the fight, Wayne McCullough was again impressed by the Dubliner's progress, and felt that the time was right for him to take a further step up in class. It seemed obvious to him that Dunne should now be tested by a seasoned, crafty and durable professional. But Brian Peters, while acknowledging that both he and Dunne had a dilemma on their hands, preferred to play the cautious card: 'Bernard has made a great start but he still has a lot to learn. Some of the American writers have been going over the top and already they are talking about Marco Antonio Barrera and Scott Harrison, but I know that he is way off that stage.'

The fact was that the journalists could speculate as much as they wanted, but Peters would make the decisions about Dunne's career, in the best interests of the boxer. Patience was indeed a virtue. Since he had been given the all-clear after his brain-scan scare, Dunne had proved his ability in the ring. He could mix it, he could hit with either hand, he had a good jab – and he had the looks and the connections. Add to that the fact that he was pure box office, possessed style and grace, had guts and bags of ability – and on top of all that, he was Irish and, therefore, was at a distinct advantage, given the large and vociferous ex-patriot community spread across the United States! The boxing world knew that there was a twenty-one-year-old Dublin featherweight destined for glory advancing through the rankings. The first six months of 2003 had been good to Bernard Dunne, and the future looked bright. A well-earned rest in Ireland was now the main priority for the man who had shown the world that, sometimes, you do get a second chance to make a first impression.

5

ONE FIGHT AT A TIME

Patience is a virtue that causes no shame
Irish proverb

With Bernard Dunne now making the headlines across the United States, the people of Ireland would be anxious to see their hottest boxing prospect perform on home turf. Dunne and Peters knew that it was just a matter of time before a fight in Dublin came around. For Peters, Bernard would be returning to Ireland for a specific reason: 'When I bring Bernard back to Dublin, I would like it to be for a title . . . . There's no point bringing him back for a small fight when he's on good money and getting great exposure in the States.'

In the background, Sugar Ray Leonard also knew that a return to Dublin was inevitable. However, with the media interest in the States growing continually, Dunne's immediate future lay with the American circuit. The sparring he was getting was second-to-none: 'Sugar' Shane

Mosley, who was preparing to fight Oscar De La Hoya for the undisputed championship of the world in the welterweight division, was prominent among his partners. In fact, Dunne's training at Roach's gymnasium was a crowd-puller in itself, with fans and journalists vying to get a look at the young Irishman. Sugar Ray wanted to keep his man's feet firmly on the ground, despite the fact that he had immense faith in Dunne's ability in the ring. 'I honestly feel that Bernard can be world champion in two years,' said Leonard. 'Everyone has been impressed with him over here. He has so much power and he knows what he wants.'

Regarding his potential when compared to the 'Clones Cyclone', five-time world champion Barry McGuigan, Leonard was sure that the Dubliner was a brighter prospect: 'At this stage of their respective careers, I would say that Bernard has more potential than Barry McGuigan. He's a puncher who can box, a boxer who can punch, and that is a rare combination.'

On his return to the Wild Card Gymnasium after his summer break, Dunne got down to some serious training. His sparring was again of the highest standard, with the IBF super-featherweight champion of the world, Carlos Hernandez, providing many testing rounds in the ring. Add to that names such as Manny Pacquiao and Willie Jorrin, and it was evident that Dunne was receiving probably the best tutoring available in the United States.

The boxing season for Dunne began again in earnest

on 3 October at the Sandia Casino in Albuquerque, New Mexico where Julio Cesar Oyuela was to provide the challenge. Dunne's opponent was a thirty-six-year-old journeyman from Honduras who came to the ring off the back of seven straight defeats. Having turned professional at the relatively late age of twenty-eight, his career was hanging by a thread as he stood in the opposite corner from the bundle of skilful energy that was Bernard Dunne. Not surprisingly, the fight, which was scheduled to go six rounds, was over in double-quick time, as Oyuela failed to appear for the second round. The first round had been enough for him. Dunne had studied his opponent well and in the opening minutes had unleashed a series of accurate body punches at Oyuela, convincing the veteran that he was out of his depth with Dunne. When the two boxers retired to their corners, Oyuela called for the referee and the doctor, claiming that his hand was hurt. It was a clever way of getting out of the fight. The bout was declared a technical knockout for Dunne, making it nine wins in nine outings. It had been little more than a three-minute sparring session: Dunne had not even broken a sweat. For Oyuela it was to be his penultimate fight, and when he was stopped in two rounds by Al Seeger three months later, he hung up his gloves for good.

The rise of Bernard Dunne was going to plan as he prepared for his tenth outing, against Alejandro Cruz, at the Desert Diamond Casino in Tucson, Arizona, on 7 November. However, Dunne was living a very lonely existence in California and homesickness was beginning to take a hold on him. Dunne's lifestyle seemed ideal, with permanent sunshine and Hollywood stars being encountered on a daily basis while he was out jogging in the avenues of Beverley Hills. But when training was over for the day, the boredom and loneliness became hard for him to deal with. It was a difficult time for Dunne, who was due to marry his fiancée, Pamela, in Dublin in January 2004. The plan was that Pamela would join him in Los Angeles, but until then, it was a case of knuckling down and sticking to the plan. There had been rumours that Sky Sports were interested in signing the Irishman on a golden handcuffs deal; given that he was halfway through his three-year contract with Sugar Ray Leonard, Dunne and Peters were keen to keep their options open. As soon as his apprenticeship was completed, it was accepted that he would return to Ireland to chase his dream and win a world title on home soil.

Fight number ten was against a man who, on paper, would provide the bare minimum of resistance to Dunne. Cruz, who was the same age as Dunne, had a record of four wins and four defeats in his eight previous fights. In his preceding bout, he had gone six rounds and enjoyed a comfortable points decision over the promising Brazilian Adriano Dos Santos, proving his durability as a fighter. Despite this, Dunne was the hottest of favourites as the men climbed into the ring.

The first round was slow to get going, as each boxer tested the relative strengths and weaknesses of his opponent. Late in the round, Dunne threw a right hand at Cruz and, on connecting, instantly recoiled as pain coursed from his hand throughout his body: he had injured his hand and was in severe pain as the bell sounded. In his corner, the situation was assessed; it was decided to let him box on. The injury was a considerable setback for Dunne. As well as the physical hindrance it presents, carrying a hand injury also has a psychological impact on a boxer. To be handicapped in the ring puts doubts in a fighter's mind and completely changes the way in which a bout is fought.

As Dunne came out for the second round, a rude awakening was in store for him. Cruz may have sensed there was something bothering Dunne, and soon caught the Dubliner while he was off-balance with a devastating left hook. For the first time in his professional career, Dunne was in trouble and, more worryingly, on the canvas: he had just entered alien territory. Stunned, embarrassed and angry, Dunne was soon up on his feet as the referee stared into his eyes. The knowledgeable fight fans and the journalists present that evening knew that the pressure was on Dunne to prove his credentials. He survived the rest of the round and, as he sat on his stool, regained his composure. He went on to take control of the fight. It was a case of class telling in the end, as he was awarded a unanimous points victory by 59–55, 58–55 and 58–55. He had fought through the pain barrier to survive and make it ten wins in a row – but he had also endured the biggest fright of his career. The world of boxing can be cruel, and Dunne knew that he had come very close to disaster. Add to that the fact that he had sustained an injury to his right hand, and it seemed that the fight with Cruz had cost him somewhat more than he had anticipated.

The concern about the injury to Dunne's right hand was to cause a bout he had lined up for December to be postponed. It was a setback to Dunne, who was scheduled to appear at New York's Madison Square Garden in a six-round clash against an opponent who was still to be finalised. The fight in New York would have given Dunne a chance to perform in front of the massive Irish-American population in the Big Apple. However, the severe bruising he had sustained to his hand meant that he was to forego this opportunity. It was now a case of resting and allowing the healing process to begin. On the brighter side, the break from the ring gave Dunne an opportunity to go home to Ireland after what had been a frantic year. More importantly, he had a date to keep in January at the Church of the Immaculate Conception in Clondalkin, with a certain Pamela Rooney.

With the nuptials completed and the vows exchanged, Bernard and Pamela began married life with a well-deserved honeymoon in the Costa del Sol. Nonetheless, boxing was not too far from their minds: Bernard was due to resume training in Los Angeles in the New Year, with a view to returning to the ring at the HP Pavilion in San Jose in early March 2004. With the hand injury seemingly on the mend, his opponent that evening was another professional in the twilight of his career, Evangelio Perez from Panama. Despite being almost thirty-six years of age, Perez had a considerable record. With forty-four fights under his belt, the Panamanian boasted a record of twenty-seven wins and seventeen defeats. A true veteran of thirteen years in the ring, he had fought Jose Bonilla for the WBA flyweight title in 1997. In March 2000, he had claimed the WBC Americas featherweight crown with a victory over the highly rated Hugo Dianzo. Perez had also been the Panamanian champion. All in all, he posed a threat to Dunne.

In spite of the scare in his last outing, Dunne was in sparkling form throughout the fight with Perez, which went the full six rounds. In the first round, Dunne landed two excellent body shots and scored with a series of combination shots after trapping Perez on the ropes. In the second, Perez's right eye began to swell, and Dunne made the situation worse for the Panamian by connecting with a succession of hard jabs, which had his opponent wincing in pain. In the next round, Dunne connected with a sweet right hand to the nose; the punch drew blood and left Perez stunned and dishevelled as the round ended. Thereafter, Dunne piled on the punishment, scoring with several blows to Perez's head. In the last minute of the sixth round, Perez was holding on for dear life; not surprisingly, Dunne was awarded the fight on a comfortable unanimous decision by the three judges.

It had been an excellent display by Dunne, and Brian

Peters was sure that an attempt to capture either the North American Boxing Federation or the North American Boxing Organisation title would be feasible before the end of 2004: 'This was another solid performance from Bernard, and the start of what will be a big year for him. It's about the right fights at the right time now, and we won't be rushed into anything. He should be in a position hopefully at the end of the year to fight for an American belt, and then move on to fight for a European title, ideally in Dublin.'

Dunne had proved that he could go the full six rounds and, more importantly, take a solid punch. He was now facing the type of opponent that he had previously yearned to take on. The 'false economy' of one-round knockouts was becoming a distant memory, as his career seemed to take a leap forward. There was to be no rest for Dunne: two weeks after the Perez bout, he found himself back at the Marconi Museum in Tustin, California, facing his next challenge – in the form of thirty-three-year-old Angelo Luis Torres from Washington State. It was a case of two steps forward, one step back for the Dubliner: this contest was a step down in class for Dunne. Torres was a relative latecomer to the fight game and had a record of nine wins, nine defeats and one draw in his nineteen fights to date. Given the calibre of his opponents, the fact that he had suffered three knockouts in his career suggested that his boxing ability was somewhat limited. Despite this, the fight went the full eight rounds – another landmark for Dunne – but the Dubliner won every round easily and was the deserved winner. It was a pyrrhic victory for Dunne, however: the injury to his right hand, which had troubled him greatly before Christmas, resurfaced after the fight. He was to wait a frustrating three months before entering the ring again.

Dunne's next outing was against another journeyman, Pedro Mora, on 2 July. A boxer such as Mora should never have been matched against someone like Dunne. With a record of four wins in thirteen fights, the Mexican came into the Dunne fight having won just once in his previous nine outings. Of his eight defeats before he entered the ring at the Pala Casino near San Diego in California, he had suffered seven knockouts and was mere cannon fodder for Dunne. Another 'chopping block'. To say the least, it was not clear what Dunne stood to gain from such an outing. However, the Mexican put up a brave show and took Dunne the full six rounds. Given the calibre of his opponent, a stoppage would have been the expected result for Dunne. With the hand injury still playing on his mind, Dunne was comfortable throughout the fight and took the fight easily, on points. In the early stages, Dunne's jab was in overdrive, and he pounded Mora with two left hooks that had the Mexican reeling. In the fourth, Dunne had his man on the canvas with an excellent right hand, but the Mexican, to his credit, refused to fold and took the fight to Dunne in the fifth. In the end, both fighters displayed their durability and the decision went to the judges.

For Dunne, the victory was his thirteenth in a row, but he and his management knew that an opponent of the class of Mora should have been dispatched with more style. Dunne's career was in danger of going round in circles. He needed an opponent that would test his ability to the full – one that would give him a real fight, as opposed to a glorified sparring session. It was then that the television show *ShoBox* came calling for Dunne again; and *ShoBox* was not in the business of screening mismatches. Accordingly, Dunne was matched with a rough-and-tumble Mexican by the name of Adrian Valdez for a showpiece event on 19 August.

On paper, Valdez seemed to be the perfect opponent for Dunne. A tough fighter, he came to the bout, at the Aldrich Arena in St Paul, Minnesota, with a record of sixteen victories – six by knockout – and only three defeats, in a paid career that had begun in August 1999. Valdez, who like Dunne was twenty-four, was another relative latecomer to the fight game, having fought just fifteen times as an amateur, winning on twelve occasions. In March 2003, Valdez won the WBC Mexican super-bantamweight title when he recorded a first-round knockout of the champion Sammy Ventura. Valdez was no journeyman, and Dunne knew that the bout would be a serious test.

There was a lot at stake for both fighters. Dunne had been named as number fifty-three in the WBA's world rankings after his win over Mora; a win over Valdez would place him in contention for a crack at a North

American title. Valdez was in a similar predicament: he was ranked in the top fifty by the WBA, was keen, hungry and durable, and had plenty of skill.

The razzmatazz was all there as Dunne entered the ring dressed in emerald green, while trainer Freddie Roach donned an oversize leprechaun's hat. Dunne was roundly cheered by the Irish supporters. As the bell to open the first round sounded, Dunne did the pressing, and put tremendous pressure on Valdez, who struck back and cut Dunne on the forehead. To be cut so early in the fight was a setback for Dunne, but he kept to the original fight plan while the cornermen dealt with the gash. The fight became a war of attrition, with Dunne's superior ability to attack giving him the edge. In the end, Dunne took the decision unanimously, on a scoreline of 97–93, 96–94 and 96–95. It had been his hardest fight in his fourteen paid outings. However, he had shown courage – and an ability to stand up and fight, particularly when Valdez opened up with a vicious combination in the ninth round. How impressive Dunne's achievement had been was reinforced two months later, when Valdez knocked out the Mexican Cesar Soto, who had fought for the WBC world title, in his next bout. Dunne still had a perfect record and was moving into the top fifty of the world ratings. A title shot looked to be on the cards. In sport, however, nobody can tell what twists and turns may lie ahead.

6

THE PRODIGAL SON RETURNS

When I die, Dublin will be written in my heart.

James Joyce

In August 2004, Crystal Palace's then-manager Iain Dowie, when describing his team's 'never say die' attitude to football, said that they possessed something which he called 'bounce-back-ability'. Strange as it may seem, the new word caught on as an apt description of a team or individual that possessed a determination to succeed in the face of numerous setbacks; in fact, there is a campaign to have Dowie's word included in the *Oxford English Dictionary*. At the same time as Dowie was inventing somewhat dubious words, Bernard Dunne was to have his own 'bounce-back-ability' tested to the full, as his career was to be turned on its head yet again. As Dunne climbed out of the ring in Minnesota on 19 August 2004, little did he know that the fight against Adrian Valdez was to be his last to be promoted by Sugar Ray Leonard.

In September 2004, Leonard dissolved his company, Sugar Ray Leonard Boxing, and Dunne became a free agent. A potential catastrophe had again visited the career of Bernard Dunne. With a fight per month guaranteed under Leonard, Dunne was now out on his own in the United States. It was time for some hard thinking: a 'Plan B' was required.

In reality, the writing had been on the wall for the organisation known as Sugar Ray Leonard Boxing. Since 2001, Sugar Ray's foray into boxing promotion had grown significantly, and he had established a respectable stable of professional boxers, but developments in the background were having an impact on the operation. In April 2004, Leonard had signed up, along with Sylvester Stallone, to oversee a new reality television show called *The Contender*. It was to be a time-consuming venture that aimed to uncover the new 'Rocky Balboa' – and would see Leonard devote less and less time to his promotional work. Add to that the fact that there had been a serious falling-out between Leonard and his business partner Bjorn Rebney (the dispute was due to go to court) and the firm's contract with ESPN had expired, and it was hardly surprising that Leonard decided to wind-up the company. As with most fall-outs in the business world, it was an acrimonious parting of the ways, with Leonard saying of Rebney: 'That guy I worked with is suing me. My company could have blossomed, but I had a cancer in my company.'

Rebney, who was the president and chief executive

of the company, hit back, blaming Leonard's decision to devote so much of his time to *The Contender* as the reason for the parting of ways: 'The best way to describe it is that I am totally devastated. I worked incredibly hard creating and building the company, and for Ray to do what he did to me and our fighters and the company is inexcusable. He turned his back on it. He had contracts and obligations to fighters and casinos and to me.'

Initially, it was thought that some of Leonard's fighters would fall in with the matchmaker Ron Katz, who had joined up with New York-based Northeast Promotions. That was not an option for Bernard Dunne, though. It had been a bitter falling-out between Leonard and his fighters and, regardless of who was to blame for the situation, the bottom line was that all the boxers involved had received serious setbacks to their careers. Initially, Dunne was asked to be one of the participants on *The Contender*, but he politely declined: he had other fish to fry, and a return to Ireland seemed to be the logical next step for him. Ireland, and Dublin in particular, had long awaited its homecoming hero. The move back to Ireland was a risk which both Peters and Dunne were prepared to take and, besides, a break from the ring was needed to ensure that Dunne's right hand was allowed to mend properly. It was also important to make sure that the momentum that Dunne had created in the United States was not lost. The opportunity was to come in the form of RTÉ, the national broadcaster. RTÉ managers indicated that they were prepared to devote prime-time television coverage to Dunne. With hindsight, it can be seen that this proposal revitalised Irish professional fighting. Lady Luck had called again, and the media in Ireland had shown their faith in Dunne. The deal was on, and Dunne was on his way back home.

As Christmas 2004 arrived, Dunne could have been forgiven for thinking that he was standing at the bottom of the boxing ladder again, with everything to prove. Ireland, Britain and Europe would offer him very different challenges. Despite the fact that he returned from the United States with an unblemished record, many boxers questioned the standard of Dunne's opponents while he had been in exile. With his apprenticeship in America at an end, Dunne gradually cut his ties with Freddie Roach; Harry Hawkins was brought in on a full-time basis to look after the Dubliner. Dunne was in very good hands: Belfast man Harry Hawkins – and indeed the Hawkins family – knows all there is to know about boxing. In Los Angeles, Roach was overseeing the career of Manny Pacquiao, but he was still keeping an eye on Dunne's progress. In due course, the date of Dunne's debut in Ireland was arranged. The venue could not have been a better one for the Neilstown fighter: the National Stadium on Dublin's South Circular Road was chosen for his contest with Jim Betts from Scunthorpe.

The Irish Amateur Boxing Association has always been a progressive organisation. In the 1930s, Ireland had been the first country in Europe to erect a purpose-built boxing arena. The National Stadium has seen some classic battles over the years, with the cream of Ireland's amateur talent having cut their teeth there. Dunne's career had been no different; now, his first paid bout back in Dublin would be on familiar territory. With a capacity of just over two thousand, coupled with a low ceiling and tiered seating, 'the Stadium' can be a formidable arena in which to perform: either exhilarating or intimidating for the boxer. Dunne was in no doubt that he would get the Dublin crowd behind him; he needed a comfortable bout to ease him into the professional scene in Ireland. Nevertheless, there was no doubt that the pressure was on Dunne. There was an air of expectation regarding his return and, of course, there was the added pressure associated with the fight being screened live by RTÉ.

Dunne could escape the glare of the Dublin fans and media as he went through his paces in the Holy Trinity Gymnasium in Belfast. While the quality of the sparring may not have been as high as in Roach's Wild Card Boxing Club, Harry Hawkins was making sure that nothing was left to chance. Speaking to Eamon O'Hara of the *Irish News*, Dunne expressed his satisfaction with his new surroundings:

'It could not be better at the minute. I'm feeling very good, strong, and the sparring has been just fantastic, as good if not better than I expected, so I am very happy with the way things are going. For myself and my family and friends, it's great to have this opportunity now after three years in America. It's an opportunity for me to show everyone what I am capable of, and then I'll take things from there. I have had a good rest period – I took three months completely off – and I haven't fought in nearly six months. So the hand is fine, it isn't causing me any problems, and it's feeling strong again, which is great. So, I am enjoying the preparations for next week, and I'm ready to get back in there again.'

For Brian Peters, everything had fallen into place perfectly. The fight fans in Dublin were eager to see Dunne back in the ring, and the bill was sold out within twenty-four hours of tickets going on sale. At twenty-five years of age, Dunne's exile in the States had not had an adverse impact on his popularity in Dublin and beyond – and he was, of course, topping the bill for the first time in his career. Still, there was a fight to be won.

Dunne's opponent, Jim Betts, was really only the window-dressing for the occasion. Betts was, to put it mildly, mediocre. Having turned professional in 1998, he had won his first twelve bouts and in 2001 had fought Nicky Booth for the British bantamweight crown. Betts had been knocked out in the seventh round of that contest, and from that point on his career had been on a steep downward curve. From 2002 to 2004, he had, through injury and apathy, been absent from the ring; he now faced Dunne having had only two competitive outings in two years. While the wise old hacks in the press box may have rolled their eyes at the apparent mismatch, Dublin had caught the boxing bug, and the fans awaited their hero.

The occasion matched the hype. The 'Olé! Olé, Olé,

Olé!' brigade was out in force as the atmosphere in the arena intensified. When the moment arrived, Dunne made his colourful entrance, to emphatic cheers. In his own corner, Betts knew that he was the main course on the menu, as Ireland tuned in to see the phenomenon that was Bernard Dunne. Referee David Irvine, from Belfast, sent the two men to their corners, and with the sound of the bell and the roar of the crowd, Bernard was back home. The fight itself was tough. The bout lasted until the fifth round, when Dunne opened up and caught his opponent with a crisp left hook to the body that winded him – and ultimately ended the contest as the referee decided that he had seen enough. Dunne did not escape unscathed from the ring, however. Betts had opened a slight cut over his left eye during the fight; Dunne later wrote it off as the result of a clash of heads. Speaking after the fight, the Dubliner praised the journeyman Betts: 'Jim was a tough opponent. I definitely needed this first fight back, and I couldn't have asked for a better performance. The crowd were fantastic and I was delighted to win in front of them.'

For Brian Peters, it had been a case of 'job done'; bigger and better nights beckoned. Speaking to the press, he told them that he was looking for a 'bigger venue' for Dunne's next fight, and added that 'we will definitely be staying in this country'.

One organisation that was most definitely interested in seeing Dunne stay in Ireland was RTÉ. Their first venture into professional boxing since the halcyon days of

Barry McGuigan in the 1980s had astounded producers: Dunne's fight had drawn an average audience of 150,000 viewers – compared with an original estimate of 100,000. Given that the fight had been screened at 10.45 PM, it was a resounding success: the coverage of the fight had gained a larger audience than similar sporting events which had been broadcast in mid-afternoon or the early evening. For RTÉ's head of sport, Glen Killane, it had been a personal triumph. He had been the man who had gambled on Bernard Dunne after asking RTÉ pundit and Kilkenny boxing legend Mick Dowling about his potential. RTÉ was keen for more, the Irish boxing fraternity was enthusiastic for more and, most importantly, Bernard Dunne, with fifteen wins and no defeats to his name, was eager for more.

Overseeing the operation was of course Brian Peters. Peters was old enough to understand how Irish professional boxing worked. He could recall the hype and adulation that had carried Barry McGuigan from the Ulster Hall in Belfast to the King's Hall, and then on to the world title at a jam-packed Loftus Road in London. In essence, he knew a good thing when he saw it, and skilfully managed the situation at hand. Also, he knew that Dunne had caught the imagination of an Irish sporting world that was crying out for a hero in the ring. With the hype surrounding Dunne growing by the day, the National Stadium was booked again for his next appearance, scheduled for 14 May. This time, an opponent with credibility in European circles was sought: the featherweight ranked number seven in Europe, Yuri Voronin from Ukraine, was chosen to be Dunne's next opponent.

The fight was promoted as Dunne's biggest test to date. His unbeaten record was his selling point; the bill was again sold out in record time. Should he be victorious, a place in the top ten of Europe's featherweight rankings awaited. For someone to have generated such hype at that stage of his career was incredible. RTÉ was again on board, and the process of turning Saturday night into a boxing extravaganza across Ireland was well under way. Voronin was no slouch: he was the reigning Ukrainian champion and a victory over Voronin would put Dunne firmly in the top ten rankings. Despite the fact that he had fought only once outside the former Soviet Union, his reputation was that of a durable fighter: he had recorded only three defeats in his twenty-seven paid outings. However, it was evident from Dunne's prefight talk that he was acquiring a growing degree of confidence that bordered on cockiness. This dubious aspect of Dunne's persona, which had been heightened by three years in the United States, had been noted by new coach Harry Hawkins at an early stage. This tendency would need to be nipped in the bud. While boasting and predictions of an opponent's demise are part and parcel of the fight game, there is an inherent danger that a boxer may have to eat his words.

In the run-up to the fight, Dunne knew that the pressure on him to perform was great, but he was confident that win number sixteen was a racing certainty: 'I am going to win, but how that happens is irrelevant. Whether it happens over ten rounds or two, it doesn't matter. As long as I am winning, that is the main thing. I expect Voronin to be tough and will prepare to go the distance. But if a chance comes up and he sticks his chin in the air, then I will take it.'

At the press conference, Dunne had other issues he wished to put straight. Ireland has always had its fair share of doom merchants, and Bernard Dunne was not to escape such begrudgers. After he had resettled in Ireland, certain sections of the press were not helpful: rumours spread that Dunne's return from the United States had shown a lack of ambition on his part. On these claims, Dunne hit back with one word: 'rubbish'. As far as he was concerned, he had no time for the naysayers of Ireland; all that had happened to him was that he 'had swapped one world-class trainer, Freddie Roach, for another, in Harry Hawkins.' The only way to stop the back-biting was for Dunne to do his talking in the ring, against Voronin.

The Ukrainian was not backwards in coming forwards in the fighting-talk stakes either. When he arrived in Dublin, he was accused of not giving Dunne the respect he deserved by taking on the fight only seven days after he had stopped his fellow countryman Nodir Kholnazaroc in seven rounds. Add to this the fact that Voronin admitted that he had never seen any footage of Dunne fighting, and it was evident that he was probably out for a pay cheque rather than glory. However, talk is cheap, and Voronin was talkative: 'Bernard is unbeaten, so I know that it will be difficult, but his previous record is irrelevant. What he and I have done before is irrelevant. What is important is what we do when we fight each other, and I have come here to win.'

For all his talk, Voronin proved in the ring that he was not there to admire the scenery: the fight went the full ten rounds. It was a brutal and bloody battle, which Dunne shaded 96–94 on referee David Irvine's scorecard. Dunne's face told the tale of the fight after the final bell. By the tenth round, it seemed that Dunne had the fight in the bag, but out of nowhere the Ukrainian unleashed a final onslaught that had Dunne reeling – and the crowd in a panic. Dunne was literally hanging on, as vicious rights and lefts rained down on his flailing defence from the southpaw. Dunne was on the way to defeat as his corner screamed at him to hang on for the rest of the round. The fight became farcical as Dunne wrestled his opponent to the ground twice in a desperate bid to stay in contention. By the end of the bout, Dunne knew he had been in a scrap, and Hawkins knew he had some work to do. It had not gone to plan, and the crowd knew it – as did the media.

The inquest was under way as the hacks tried to piece together what had gone wrong from Dunne's perspective. There were no headlines such as 'Dunne Deal' or 'Dunne and Dusted' in the papers the following morning as reality hit home. Writing in the *Irish Sun* on 16 May, Neil O'Riordan pointed out that you could take either a positive or a negative from Dunne's performance. He added: 'The Ukrainian came oh-so-close to derailing the Dunne bandwagon in the tenth and final round with a shuddering left which had the favourite floundering. Another couple of lefts had Dunne in real trouble and on the ropes before he regrouped and realised that all he had to do was stay away from Voronin until the bell sounded.'

The doubts had been planted in the minds of the faithful. For Peters, it was obvious that Dunne was having difficulty dealing with brawlers. In professional boxing, there is only so much that can be gleaned from sparring with the top professionals. While it looks good on paper, it counts for very little under the spotlights in the heat of battle, when a seasoned battler uses all his guile to frustrate an opponent. When Voronin opened up in the last round, he exposed Dunne as someone who lacked the experience to 'mix it' – or, more importantly, to stay out of trouble. There was still a lot of work to be done. For all his exertions, Dunne had picked up five cuts to the face during the bout. It was a painful experience for Dunne, who paid tribute to his opponent after the fight. Also, more ominously, referee David Irvine revealed that at one stage in the last round, the notion of stopping the fight to save Dunne had crossed his mind: Dunne had literally been a solid punch away from defeat. However, as it stood, Dunne's record was fought sixteen, won sixteen. The 'bounce-back-ability' had come back into the equation.

The summer break came at the right time for Dunne;

his next fight was scheduled for October 2005. During that time, he made the decision to drop a weight to super-bantamweight, and left behind the featherweight scene. He would need to shed at least four pounds to come inside the new limit, but it was a task that he felt comfortable about achieving. In the European super-bantamweight division, the man to catch was Hartlepool's Michael Hunter. The twenty-eight-year-old southpaw had claimed the British title in 2004 with an impressive victory over the then-champion Mark Payne. A year later, he had added the Commonwealth and European crowns to his name after shading a majority verdict over Esham Pickering in his home town (a decision that was widely disputed). Hunter was in the sights of the Dunne camp, and a further victory against somebody of Hunter's class would make Dunne the leading contender for a crack at the European crown. The man chosen was Noel Wilders from Castleford, who had lost a tough battle with the aforementioned Esham Pickering three months before his date with Dunne. While he would offer Dunne the type of stiff resistance that the Dubliner needed in the run-up to a crack at Hunter's European title, the fight fell through when Wilders, who was said to be contemplating retirement, withdrew at the last minute. Given that the International Boxing Council's version of the featherweight belt was to have been at stake, the withdrawal was a major blow to both Dunne and Peters.

In the alphabet soup of professional boxing titles, the IBC crown was not what one could call prestigious. Still,

Dunne fighting for a title would add to the attraction of a bill, and the credibility of having a title would give Dunne added bargaining power in his search for glory. However, an opponent was needed. Into the equation came Sean 'Short Fuse' Hughes, from Yorkshire, who gladly made himself available for the date left vacant by the withdrawal of Wilders. On paper, Hughes was a boxer of note. After turning professional in 2002, he won his first eight fights. In March 2005, he fought Michael Hunter for the British title. He lost that fight when he was knocked out in the sixth round of the scheduled twelve, but he had proved that he possessed a fair degree of class. He would surely test Dunne. The doubts in the minds of the boxing fraternity concerning Dunne's potential had still to be appeased: the pressure was on Dunne as 14 October approached.

It was labelled as 'Judgement Day' for Bernard Dunne, and the National Stadium sold out in double-quick time. The chief supporting contest that Friday evening would see fellow Dubliner Jim Rock go toe-to-toe with Welshman Alan Jones for the vacant IBC middleweight crown. This bout was indeed a grudge match, as Jones had shaded a decision over 'The Pink Panther' Rock in 2003 at the Ulster Hall in Belfast. Add to that the fact that Brian Magee, Oisin Fagan, Paul Griffin, Paul Hyland and Stephen Haughian all had bouts scheduled on the bill, and a truly mouth-watering night was in store. Again RTÉ carried the fight live, as Dunne aimed to purge the 'blip' of the last round against Voronin. Again, he was expressing confidence as the fight drew near: 'Obviously if I can stop him early, I will be delighted, but getting a win is my first priority. You don't get paid by the hour in this game, so obviously if you get your work done early, that's a bonus.'

Having agreed to meet Dunne only four days before the fight, it was inevitable that Sean Hughes was to be mere cannon fodder. And that is the way it went, as referee Paul Thomas intervened halfway through the second round to stop the fight in order to save Hughes from further punishment. The first round had been all Dunne's. In the second, he waited for his chance and caught the Yorkshireman with a sweet right hook, to send him flailing. Thereafter, sensing that a knockout was on the cards, Dunne unleashed a merciless barrage of punches that forced the referee to act. It was over; Dunne had passed the 'Judgement Day' test, and he had a belt around his waist to prove it. To add to the glory, Jim Rock made it a fantastic night for Dublin boxing by avenging his defeat in October 2003 to Alan Jones and claiming the IBC belt at middleweight. Things were looking up again for both Dunne and Irish boxing.

7

EUROPEAN ADVENTURES

A change is as good as a rest.
Traditional proverb

With a fight with European champion Michael Hunter edging ever closer, Bernard Dunne's next foray into the ring took him to Leipzig in Germany. His opponent on 10 December 2005, Marian Leondraliu from Romania, was not expected to pose any great difficulty to Dunne: the eastern European had lost fourteen of his twenty-seven professional fights. (Dunne's opponent was meant to have been Togo's Daniel Kodjo Sassou, who had, in-auspiciously, lost his opening six fights as a professional. When an offer was received for Sassou to fight Sergio Blanco in Barcelona at the same time as the proposed bout with Dunne, Sassou opted to forego the fight in Leipzig.) Leondraliu was ranked 120 places further down the European ladder than Dunne and was out of his depth. Brian Peters was keen to build up the reputation of the Romanian, pointing out that he had fought against 'world-rated' boxers such as France's Souleymane 'The Sensation' M'Baye and Uzbekistan's Mohamad Abdulaev, adding that the fact that M'Baye was the mandatory challenger to Ricky Hatton's titles showed his pedigree. The bill that night in the Leipzig Arena was headed by the IBF middleweight title fight between the Armenian Arthur Abraham and the Nigerian Kingsley Ikeke; 6 million viewers were expected to tune in across Europe. Despite the fact that Dunne's fight was part of the undercard, RTÉ again chose to cover the fight live, with a two-hour programme scheduled for the evening.

The fight went to plan, and Dunne stopped his man in the sixth round. He now had a perfect record of eighteen wins in eighteen fights. The fight had been portrayed in the media as a potential banana skin, but this proved to be wide of the mark. The end came at the halfway point of the sixth, when Dunne landed a powerful left hook into Leondraliu's ribs, bringing him to his knees; the referee quickly decided to stop the fight. Dunne had received another bloodied face for his endeavours, when his right eye was opened in an accidental clash of heads during the fourth round. While he had fought on only three occasions during 2005, the victory over Leondraliu was a satisfactory end to the year for Dunne; 2006 promised to be a defining year for the Dubliner.

Regarding Dunne's progress, there were rumblings of discontent among the media that inertia had set in. In reality, if you have a boxer that has captured the public imagination, there is no point in risking his credibility by placing him in the ring against tricky opponents. There is too much money at stake. However, the fact was that, four years after turning professional, Dunne had been matched with a fighter who could well have been chosen as an opponent in his novice days.

Writing in the *Sunday Times* on 18 December, Dave Hannigan suggested that both the Dunne camp and RTÉ might be heading down the 'same sorry path' that the BBC had done with Audley Harrison, the 2000 Olympic heavyweight champion. Harrison had taken the gold medal at the Sydney Olympics in the super-heavyweight division. On his arrival home, the BBC, who had lost all of its professional boxing coverage to Sky Sports and ITV, signed Harrison on a £1 million contract in return for the right to screen his first ten paid fights. While there was a genuine belief that Harrison would eventually go on to win a world title, his early fights were over-hyped, glorified sparring contests with an assortment of jour-neymen – in essence, not the type of fighters that Olympic champions should meet. As the BBC had committed to ten fights, there was no point in risking Harrison against tough opponents, and Harrison's career stalled. The bottom line is that it's easy to be a star in the ring if you are fighting nobodies.

Hannigan went to town on the Bernard Dunne phenomenon, suggesting that he should never even have contemplated a fight with Leondraliu. He pointed out that the Romanian had lost ten of his previous thirteen outings and that Dunne needed some 'credible opponents'. Hannigan made a stinging attack: 'Nobody is questioning Dunne's enormous potential, and anyone with a love for the sport must be satisfied by the way he has invigorated crowds in Dublin. Unfortunately, there comes a point in every fighter's development when he must prove capable of more than summary dispatches of stiffs.' Hannigan ended his article by suggesting that the television ratings for Dunne's fights were the reason why he was pitched against 'nobodies'. 'Something has to give,' he concluded.

The bandwagon rolled on relentlessly, however: Bernard's next contest was announced in a blaze of publicity at the Burlington Hotel in Dublin just before Christmas. Back into the equation came the battling southpaw Noel Wilders from Castleford in England. This was the same Wilders who had withdrawn from a fight with Dunne for the IBC super-bantamweight crown in October 2004. The bout offered Dunne the chance to prove his point himself against a fighter who had been the British and European bantamweight champion as well as losing out for the WBO crown in 2004 to the marvellously named Silence Mabuza in South Africa. While Wilders had lost three of his four previous bouts before he met Dunne, and had come out of retirement to fight the Irishman, nobody could deny his class. All the same, this was definitely a stepping stone for Dunne. Also on the card for the bill at the National Stadium on 26 January were Brian Magee and, in a mouth-watering clash for the Irish lightweight title, Dubliner Michael Gomez and Peter McDonagh from Galway. As usual, tickets went like hot cakes.

Christmas and New Year were effectively cancelled in Bernard Dunne's house as he sought to keep himself in prime condition for the fight in late January. Dunne knew that he had something to prove about his career to the whisperers and snipers, and he left nothing to chance. A big performance was needed and, with live television again the order of the day, he had to deliver. The press conference and weigh-in before the fight were held in the Burlington Hotel. When Wilders came in at slightly over the weight limit, he had to perform a public 'Full Monty' to make the nine stone maximum weight. Wilders admitted that he had only five weeks of serious training behind him going into the ring; compared to Dunne's fitness, he was at a severe disadvantage. However, he advised the press that he was 'ready' and that he had 'the buzz again'. He asserted that, if he could beat Dunne, he could place himself right back in contention for a crack at Michael Hunter's European title. The fight was essentially a final eliminator for the European title and, as such, was to be a crucial test for Dunne.

The atmosphere in the stadium that night approached fever pitch as yet again the Dublin boxing fraternity got behind their hero. The fight went only six rounds, and Dunne put in a performance of consummate class. The crowd in the National Stadium lapped it up and cried out for more. In the end, Dunne had the skill and speed to exploit Wilders's defensive tactics and proved that he was definitely a boxer on the up. In the sixth round, Dunne sensed victory and opened up on Wilders with a series of combinations that left him on the back foot. A stinging right hook to the ribs floored the Englishman, but he scrambled to his feet, and referee David Irvine nodded for the fight to continue. Like a terrier in a rabbit hole, Dunne went for his prey with great purpose, and within seconds Irvine had stepped in to call it a day on behalf of Wilders.

On the Monday after the fight, the *Sun*'s Tomas Rohan opened his piece by writing: 'Noel Wilders took a battering from Bernard Dunne – and then tipped him for European glory.' Once again, Dunne had scars to show for his endeavours: a clash of heads in the third round had opened up the old wound above his right eye. This, however, was not to detract from the win, which put Dunne in pole position for a crack at the European title. Understandably, Dunne was happy with his performance: 'I am still learning, but I think that it was a good result against a fighter of Noel's calibre. He is a tough guy and he showed all his experience in there tonight. He has been European champion, so it's a good scalp for me and a great name to have on my record.'

Brian Peters was certain that the European super-bantamweight belt would be Bernard's that year, but there was a pecking order when it came to getting a crack at the title. Hunter had two fights lined up in the interim; Dunne had to be patient. A boxer who is out of the ring for an extended period of time will quickly go stale, and it was considered wise to get a couple of extra fights under Dunne's belt in preparation for his eventual date with Hunter. It was time for Dunne to travel once again: the Italian town of Piedmont was to be the venue for Bernard's next dust-up, with Sergio Santillan as the unlikely opponent, on 3 April.

The fight was to be known as the 'Italian Job', with Santillan – who had a record of twenty wins, six losses and three draws – in theory providing a reasonable test for Dunne. But again, the critics had their knives sharpened. In the *Sunday Times*, Sue Denham twisted the knife in RTÉ and Bernard Dunne by pointing out the shortcomings of Santillan and questioning RTÉ's billing of the fight as 'implausibly, a serious test for Dunne'. Denham went on to point out that the native Argentinian was ranked 113th in the world and had not won a bout outside his home country. He had also won only three of his last nine contests. Denham took great delight in pointing out that the fight, fixed for 3 April, should have been held on April Fool's Day instead. While there was an element of facetiousness in the criticism of Dunne's opponent, Denham was saying out loud what various members of the Irish boxing fraternity were thinking. In essence, Dunne needed a test against a world-class opponent, and no 'window dressing' of the bout by RTÉ – who had invested serious money in Dunne – could detract from that fact. The reality was that Dunne needed to move up a level and Santillan was not going to provide him with anything other than a glorified sparring match.

In the event, the fight, Dunne's twentieth professional outing, went the full eight rounds. It was not the emphatic win that the Dubliner had hoped for, but it still kept him at the top of the queue for a crack at the European title. In what was described as an 'entertaining contest', Dunne displayed great skill in both attack and defence. With just over a minute gone in the first round, Dunne caught Santillan with a sweet right hand to the head that knocked him to the canvas. Credit must go to the Argentinian for his bravery: he climbed to his feet and began to mix it with the Dubliner. Dunne was within his comfort zone, however, and scored with ease throughout. In the last round, a stumble by Dunne saw him fall to the canvas, but this was the only blemish in an assured performance. Yet again, Dunne sustained a nasty-looking cut above his right eye; the reoccurrence of this injury was a cause for concern in the Dunne camp.

Despite being nicknamed 'The Tiger', Santillan had been well beaten. Now, the Irish public yearned for Dunne to step into the ring against the European champion Michael Hunter. The Dunne bandwagon was in danger of stalling; Dunne waited for his chance.

Rumours began circulating in early May that the Point Depot in Dublin had been booked for mid-October. The reigning European champion had proved his credibility as a champion by successfully defending his title on two occasions. The Dunne v. Hunter clash was a mouth-watering prospect. The Hartlepool-based Hunter had made it known that he was willing to travel to Dublin, and the autumn date seemed to have been agreed in principle by the two camps. With the title fight still six months away, Dunne was matched with the twenty-two-year-old American David Martinez in another test at the Point on 3 June. Again, the fight was to be broadcast live on RTÉ. With a record of fifteen wins, one loss and one draw, Martinez has no mean boxer. Moreover, the American was talking up his prospects, saying that he was in the mood to take away Bernard's unbeaten record and adding that, in defeating Dunne, he would teach him more about boxing than he had learned in his previous twenty outings. Dunne, as usual, remained determined and focused before the bout, saying that he would study the videos of Martinez in order to prepare for his twenty-first paid bout.

Martinez held the rather grand nickname of 'El Finito' – 'The Terminator'. He was considered to be a competent fighter who could roll with the punches but did not possess a significant punch himself. He had turned professional at the tender age of eighteen after an impressive amateur career in which he had claimed four American amateur titles and a gold medal at the Junior Olympic Games. His only defeat in the paid game had come when he was forced to retire with a nasty cut in the tenth round of a brutal clash with Tomas Villa in July 2005. That defeat was his only loss in his professional career. Now, he saw the clash with Dunne as a gilt-edged chance to storm his way on to the world super-bantamweight stage.

In his preparations for the fight, Martinez had sparred with former world champion Johnny Tapia. Tapia had been world champion at three weights and had sparred with Dunne on numerous occasions. Martinez would go in against Dunne with the knowledge that he had been afforded the best preparations and would be aware of Dunne's fighting style. Dunne, the 'Irish Rover', was right to be wary of the American as he came to Dublin in a confident and hungry state of mind.

There may have been another reason why the American was exuding confidence. Two weeks after Dunne was to face Martinez, Pamela was due to give birth to the couple's first child: it might be difficult for Dunne to concentrate on the job at hand on 3 June. The roles were reversed in the Dunne household as, instead of worrying about Bernard in the run-up to a fight, as was the norm before a fight, all the care and attention was lavished on Pamela.

The weigh-in for the fight took place in Tallaght's Plaza Hotel. Martinez was in fine fettle as he told the assembled press that he had only agreed to fight Dunne in an attempt to get his career back on track. He added that if it had not been for his defeat to Tomas Villa, he would not have been in Dublin preparing to face Dunne. His promoter, Lenny Fresquez, was more forthright in his criticism of the Dubliner, saying that Dunne was 'a nothing fighter who had only fought bums and has-beens'.

Despite this megaphone diplomacy, the Dunne camp was assured and collected in its response. Brian Peters had great pleasure in pointing out that Dunne had never been beaten in Dublin in eighty-nine amateur and four professional outings, while Dunne himself stated: 'He's going to be walking into the ring in my own home town to face me. I'll show him what I can do. If I get the chance, I will take it, and attack has always been my best defence. I just hope that my wife doesn't go into labour at the same time – although maybe that would mean a double celebration. But there's only one way that I can see this fight turning out. I am going to win, and I have no negative thoughts on it.'

The fight now bordered on a grudge contest, with no love lost between the two protagonists. A packed Point Depot awaited the action, and the Dublin crowd cheered and chanted as Dunne stepped into the ring to face the man who had belittled his talent. The early rounds were cautious, with Martinez using his reach advantage to keep Dunne at a distance. However, Bernard soon settled to his task and scored with some accurate and stinging punches that knocked the American out of his stride. There was an element of niggle between the two fighters, with referee David Irvine having to step in as some verbal abuse threatened to boil over. Still, it seemed that Martinez was getting more riled with the situation, as Dunne took things in his stride. Patience was the game, and Dunne won every one of the first seven rounds with consummate ease. By the eighth, Dunne's constant barrage of punches became too much for the American and, fifty-seven seconds into the round, his corner threw in the towel. Win number twenty-one was in the end a polished and assured performance which proved that idle talk outside the ropes is no use to a fighter once he steps inside them. Martinez left the ring that night with his tail firmly between his legs. Despite the Martinez fight being considered Dunne's most impressive display as a professional, Harry Hawkins was keen to play down the win and not to overhype his protégé. He added that he was unhappy that Dunne had let his guard down 'too much for his own good' and pointed out that there was still a lot of work to do.

After the fight, the public were longing for the clash with Hunter. There could be no more procrastination: Dunne needed the European belt around his waist in order to retain his credibility. As expected, two became three in the Dunne household, as Caoimhe was born in late June. The joy surrounding the new arrival was soon to be replaced with the reality that Dunne, Ireland's greatest prospect since the mid-1980s, had a job to do in the ring. The boxer was ready, but there were to be a few more twists along the way.

8

THE TIME FOR TALKING IS OVER

'BLOODBATH AS BERNIE GRABS BELT'
The Sun, *13 November 2006*

In the European super-bantamweight division, reigning champion Michael Hunter was truly setting the pace. On 23 June 2006, the Hartlepool-born puncher successfully defended his European title against Tuncay Kaya in Blackpool. The twenty-eight-year-old produced a gritty performance and wore down Kaya before dropping the French fighter in the ninth round with a powerful left hook to the ribs. It was his third successful defence of his crown and he was now a serious contender for a world-title shot. With Europe having been conquered, a fight with Bernard Dunne was viewed by Hunter's team as potentially a backward step, and the prospect of Hunter relinquishing his title in search of higher glory remained a distinct possibility. Speaking to the BBC after his victory over Kaya, Hunter was boisterous, saying that he had the confidence to fight anyone: 'I can raise my game to world level. Tuncay was up to the European level of fighters and that is what I have to overcome if I am going to go on from here. I don't get involved in that side of things; I just turn up and fight who is put in front of me. But I am not scared of anyone – I never have been. I will fight anyone, any time. If they bring me a world champion, I'll fight him.'

Back in Ireland, Bernard Dunne was not slow in pointing out his own claims to the European title, telling Hunter that he couldn't call himself the best super-bantamweight in Europe until he had faced 'the undefeated Irish boxer'. He added that he would have no problem meeting Hunter in Hartlepool if he had to. With the diplomatic war under way, Brian Peters entered into talks with Hunter's team with a view to securing the fight in Dublin that autumn. In the end, the talks came to nothing when, in September, Hunter decided to relinquish his European crown after having secured a crack at Canada's Steve Molitor for the IBF super-bantamweight crown in Hartlepool. Once again, as one door closed, another one opened for Dunne.

Immediately, the two names thrown into the frame for a crack at the vacant title were those of Dunne and Esham Pickering. This was the same Esham Pickering who had dropped Michael Hunter to the canvas twice in their European-title fight in 2005, only to lose on points. He was nobody's fool and, for Dunne, it would be time to deliver. Accordingly, the ruling body of the European

Boxing Union pencilled Dunne and Pickering's names in to meet for the vacant European title, with a deadline for purse bids from the promoters to secure the fight set for noon on 11 October in Rome. The fight was duly secured by Brian Peters and fixed for the Point Depot, on 11 November, with RTÉ securing the live television and a packed and partisan house guaranteed. Brian Peters predicted that the thirty-year-old Pickering would offer Dunne 'the acid test' and, indeed, his 'moment of truth'. Peters went on to put the fight in its context: 'It's a great fight for both guys and in effect it is a world-title eliminator because the winner will most likely go on to fight for a world title. It's a big night for Bernard because he will be bidding to become the first Dubliner to win a European title, and fighting at the Point he is following in the footsteps of Wayne McCullough, Steve Collins, Lennox Lewis and 'Prince' Naseem Hamed.'

The fight with Pickering was to be Dunne's toughest test to date. If he could not take the vacant European title, all his previous victories would count for nothing. Former world featherweight champion Barry McGuigan cautioned that Pickering was going to prove to be a very difficult opponent. The 'Clones Cyclone' called the fight a 50:50 encounter; for Dunne, going into the ring with an equal would be a new departure in his professional career.

The Brendan Ingle-trained Esham Pickering was thirty years of age when the match with Bernard Dunne was organised. He was perhaps past his best but he possessed a record of note. He had turned professional in 1996 and enjoyed an unblemished record in his first eleven fights. However, his first defeat came in his twelfth outing, when he lost to John Jo Irwin in a contest for the British featherweight title. Despite this setback, Pickering proved his credentials by dropping to bantamweight and winning his next six contests, to secure a crack at Mauricio Martinez for the WBO bantamweight crown in December 2000. Topping the bill that evening was Joe Calzaghe, who was to reclaim his WBO super-middleweight crown with an eleventh-round stoppage of Richie Woodall. However, for Pickering, his fight proved to be a step too far: in only his nineteenth paid outing, he lasted a mere seventy-two seconds against the Panamanian. In fact, it was a disastrous outing for Pickering, who went down for a count of six within a minute and had not fully recovered when referee Rudy Battle allowed the action to recommence. Pickering was duly caught clean by a long, sweeping right hand which sent him crashing heavily on his side. It was a hard lesson for Pickering, who had been humiliated in front of a vociferous home crowd at the Sheffield Arena.

After his devastating defeat to Martinez, Pickering's career could well have floundered, or indeed ended. Yet he went on to show his undoubted class and, in July 2003, knocked out Brian Carr to take the British super-bantamweight title in Glasgow's Braehead Arena. Pickering went from strength to strength and in January 2004 added the European title to his list of honours with a tenth-round stoppage of Italy's Vincenzo Gigliotti in Bradford. Pickering had shown flashes of brilliance in his defeat of the crouching Italian, who had twice gone the distance in world-title bids; the Briton was at the pinnacle of his career.

In October 2005, Pickering put his Commonwealth and European titles on the line against the British champion Michael Hunter in a winner-takes-all battle. It was a virtual war, and had the frenzied crowd on its feet throughout. The two warriors had a future world title as a prize, and the packed arena in Hartlepool witnessed an epic battle, which Hunter shaded, on a majority verdict – to the delight of the home crowd. For Pickering, it was again a case of hard medicine; the long road back beckoned once again. Despite the narrow loss, the truth is that you do not become a bad boxer overnight and, in December 2005, Pickering's career resumed with a victory over Fred Bonifai in Nottingham. Pickering possessed class in abundance, and the fight with Dunne would give him a prime opportunity to prove that point.

The hype surrounding the bout was unprecedented in modern times. The seven thousand tickets available for the Point Depot sold quickly, with the managing director of Ticketmaster Ireland, Eamonn O'Connor, saying that the demand had been comparable to what could be expected for a big-name band. There was a great buzz around Dublin as the big night approached. In the opposite corner, Pickering's trainer, Brendan Ingle, would be the only Dubliner not wanting to see Dunne take the crown; he was keen to talk up the fight. Ingle had been born and raised in the tough Ringsend area of Dublin and from his Sheffield gym had guided both 'Prince' Naseem Hamed and Johnny Nelson to world titles. Ingle saw the fight as being too close to call. However, he felt that his man had the edge when it came to experience and that this would work to his advantage. In putting the importance of the fight in its true context, he added: 'I'm not taking anything away from Bernard Dunne, though. Every time I see him he seems to be improving in leaps and bounds, so I know it won't be easy for us. There's a world title at stake for the winner, so we can't afford to slip up. This fight is effectively a world-title eliminator.'

Brendan Ingle's pedigree as a boxing coach is second to none in Britain and Ireland. However, he did indulge in mind games in the run-up to the fight by advising the Irish fans 'not to blink on Saturday night, you'll miss a man getting knocked out'. He added that, while a knock-out by Pickering could come early in the fight, he suggested that, 'realistically, it would happen about the sixth or seventh'. This spat of 'verbals' is part of the professional game and was to be expected. However, Dunne's coach, Harry Hawkins, knew that Pickering would pose serious questions to the 'Irish Rover', and the preparations in the Holy Trinity Gym were long and arduous. The time for talking was over: a plan was needed and the Dunne team completed their preparations. In essence, they were training to go the full distance against a gritty and shrewd pugilist.

The weigh-in drew the fans and media in their droves to the Burlington Hotel, where just four ounces in favour of Dunne separated the fighters on the scales. In a classic show of loyalty to Dunne, the Dublin bookmakers made the Neilstown man favourite, despite the fact that Pickering had held the European belt for two years. On the morning of the fight, the headlines in the Irish papers spelt out the reality of the fight to Dunne. The *Irish Mirror* screamed 'IT'S MAKE OR BREAK FOR BERNARD', while the *Irish Sun* carried the words of Ingle with a report under the headline 'YOU'LL GET DUNNE, BERN!' The *Irish Times*, however, was more pragmatic, saying simply: 'POINT DUTY IS CRUCIAL FOR DUNNE'. It was now or never for Dunne – a man who had, quite simply, captured the hearts of the Irish public.

On the eve of the fight, Michael Hunter, the former European champion, lost out to Canada's Steve Molitor in what *Boxing News* described as a 'gutsy' challenge for the IBF world super-bantamweight crown. Hunter's unbeaten record was lost in front of a vociferous home crowd in Hartlepool. For both Dunne and Pickering, the ante had been raised again: the European belt would surely put the winner high up the pecking order in his quest for a crack at a world crown.

On Saturday evening, the country tuned in as the Point Depot filled to capacity in expectation of a classic. As the moment approached, the drama of Dunne's arrival sent the crowd into a frenzy. Appearing through the dry ice, to the air of the Pogues and the Dubliners 1987 version of the 'Irish Rover', Dunne looked calm and collected as he made his way to the ring. The anthems were sung, and respected, and the introductions were made to a wall of noise that reverberated around the arena. The ring emptied; it was time for Dunne to deliver.

After a busy opening round, Pickering scored with a good right in the second that put Dunne temporarily on the back foot. However, roared on by the crowd, Dunne recovered, to pin Pickering to the ropes with a flurry of punches that was only interrupted by the bell to end the round: the manic crowd stood as one and applauded their hero. By the fifth round, Dunne was again in the ascendancy. A vicious right hand caught Pickering clean on the nose and drew blood from the Newham man. The fight was turning into a brutal and bloody brawl, with both men refusing to give an inch. Dunne's tendency to drop his guard allowed Pickering to score with some quick jabs and crosses and, as the fight reached its mid-point, it was too close to call.

In the seventh round, Pickering opened up again and connected with a stinging right. As the fight edged towards its conclusion, Pickering's growing ability to find his range looked ominous for Dunne. At the start of the eighth, Dunne was again caught by Pickering's accurate right hand; he was forced to seek the sanctuary of the ropes to avoid the onslaught. It was now time for Dunne to change plan as Pickering's class began to dictate the direction of the fight. Dunne hung in, however, and began to counter and score, as both fighters visibly tired.

A big last round was needed by the Dubliner to secure the title. He needed to dig deep; he hoped that the seven thousand spectators present would give him that extra edge. In the twelfth and final round, the blood-spattered Dunne indeed found the extra stamina that he needed to see him home. A swift right hand had Pickering in trouble, while left jabs added to his woes. Dunne fired home flurry after flurry of punches as the crowd roared him on to victory. As the final bell sounded, there was prolonged applause for the two men, who had served up a true classic. Hugs and handshakes were the order of the day, as the two bloodied and exhausted warriors returned to their corners.

The crowd now waited expectantly as the scorecards were totted up, checked and rechecked by the referee, Massino Barrovecchio. The moment of truth soon arrived, and Mike Goodhall, the master of ceremonies, lifted his microphone to announce the verdict. It was a unanimous verdict. Judge Freddie Christensen scored the contest 117–111; judge Jean-Louis Legland also scored the contest 117–111; while judge Heinrich Muehmert called it closer, with a score of 115–113 – all three in favour of the new super-bantamweight champion of Europe: Bernard Dunne. Cue mass hysteria in the ring, in the arena and in countless homes and bars across Ireland. Dunne had delivered the goods and was now ranked within the top-ten of the four major world bodies. He stood on the threshold of a shot at the world title. He had dispatched a truly worthy opponent and was thoroughly pleased with his night's work: 'It's like Christmas come early for me really, but it took an awful lot of hard work to get here. I've hardly seen my baby daughter for the last few weeks and I've night feeds to catch up on. The European title isn't the only thing on my list; I want to bring a world title back to Dublin, so hopefully this is just the first of some really big nights here.'

The prospect of bigger nights in bigger Dublin venues, such as Croke Park, now seemed likely. Dunne was fast becoming an Irish sporting phenomenon. Brian Peters, doing his job, played down the prospect of an immediate world-title shot. He told the assembled media: 'Bernard will mop up Europe in 2007 and then we'll look at the world stage; we won't be rushed into anything. A rematch with Esham is a possibility, but there are some guys on the Continent, like the Spanish fighters Kiko Martinez and Miguel Mallon.'

On the night of 11 November, Dunne became only the seventh Irishman to claim a European boxing crown. He had followed in the footsteps of Barry McGuigan, who had claimed the featherweight title at Belfast's King's Hall in November 1983; less than two years later, McGuigan was world champion. The future looked bright for Bernard Dunne as 2006 drew to a close.

9

LORDING IT OVER EUROPE

And I have promises to keep,
And miles to go before I sleep.

Robert Frost

As Bernard Dunne was soon to learn, having a European belt to your name in no way guarantees a quiet life. In simple terms, he was almost the biggest thing to hit Dublin since the invention of penicillin. He was an idol in a city that truly worships its heroes. The good times were rolling as Christmas 2006 turned into the New Year of 2007. Dunne was on a break from the ring and taking stock of how far he had come, as well as of how far he still had to go. Soon even a trip to the shops for the Dunne family became an event in itself, as everyone wanted to shake Bernard's hand or slap his back and say 'Well done!' Radio and television shows, newspaper interviews, functions, prize nights and appearances at all sorts of events became the order of the day. Signing autographs became an occupational hazard for Bernard Dunne; it was the price of fame. To the man and woman in the streets of the capital, he was their champion – and he was soon going to be the champion of the world. For Bernard, the hard work was beginning to provide dividends in both prestige and financial terms. Boxing, though, is a fickle sport and, as many former heroes can verify, fame and adulation can be taken from you in the most abrupt fashion. Enjoy the good times while they last, as the future can be cruel. For Dunne, the hard work of defending his title lay ahead in 2007. As everyone knows, it takes a very good man to win a title; but, in many cases, it takes a great man to defend and retain it.

The country of Kazakhstan has come in for some unfair publicity of late due in kind to the comedian Sacha Baron Cohen's character Borat. However, Yersin Jailauov from the former Soviet republic, who was to be Dunne's first challenger for his belt, was no fool. In theory, a boxer's first defence of a title should be a relatively straightforward affair, but Jailauov had the potential to pose some tricky questions to the Irishman. In truth, the Kazakhstani had been an exceptional amateur who, in 1998, had claimed a gold medal in the flyweight division at the prestigious Goodwill Games at Madison Square Garden. Having turned professional in 2000, the thirty-year-old challenger was, perhaps, just past his best. In March 2006, he had challenged Michael Hunter for his European belt and had been stopped in the second round in what was a controversial end to the fight. The

Hartlepool champion had controlled the first round and, early in the second, rocked Jailauov with a right hook. Despite being shaken by the punch, Jailauov seemed capable of continuing, however referee Erkki Meronen stepped in to stop the contest. The press, the spectators and both fighters were surprised by the seemingly premature stoppage, but Hunter was still champion. Afterwards, Jailauov criticised everyone except himself for his dismal performance. A clash with Dunne offered a prime opportunity for Jailauov to prove a point.

Dunne's popularity in Ireland had been founded on the strength of live television coverage. On the night he lifted the European crown, an unprecedented audience of five hundred thousand viewers tuned in to witness the drama. In winning the title against Pickering, Dunne had silenced (at least for the time being) the doubters, who had criticised the dubious calibre of opponent that Dunne had been used to. The fact remained that one loss had the potential to bring Dunne's career crashing down, so there were to be no risks taken in the ring against Jailauov. The fight was scheduled for the Point Depot on Sunday 25 March. As usual, the arena, which held seven thousand people, was a sell-out in no time at all. There was no other boxer in Europe, apart from the irresistible Ricky Hatton, who could claim to have the drawing power of Dunne. The phenomenon that was Bernard Dunne was taking on a life of its own, with rumours abounding that Croke Park – the eighty-two-thousand-seater headquarters of the GAA in north Dublin – was being earmarked as a potential venue for a world-title shot. That, however, was in the future; in the meantime, there was a fight to be fought and won with Yersin Jailauov. The emotion and glory of the victory over Esham Pickering would have been for nothing if Dunne could not cement his position as Europe's number one by dispatching the challenger from Kazakhstan.

As usual, Dunne was in a buoyant mood prior to the bill, as he happily showed off seven-month-old Caoimhe to the assembled press. Telling the media that he was 'ready to put on a show' and that he was 'on his way to the top, and the boxing business better sit up and take notice', Bernard predicted that he would 'take the guy out' at the first opportunity he got, given that he had been working hard on his strength and power. However, while Dunne was prepared to talk a good fight and predict the demise of his opponent, others began to suggest that such talk was tempting fate. In response, Dunne was adamant in his reply to the critics: 'People may think that I am cocky, but it's not that, as I am only there to have fun.'

'Boxing is show business, and it's a sport, and when I go out there I want to put on a show and I want to show people what I can do,' Dunne continued. 'I know when I can let loose and showboat, but I'm there to win and I won't let anything get in the way of that.'

On the night in question, the expectation in the arena was of a Dunne win, and a convincing one at that. Both fighters had tipped the scales at eight stone nine and a half pounds, with Dunne two inches taller than his opponent. The Irish fighter had in his favour the height, the reach, the crowd and, most importantly, the belt around his waist. Dunne's entrance was again dramatic, as the nation tuned in to see their new hero. The crowd erupted as Dunne again appeared through the dry ice into the arena. The roars subsided and the familiar 'Olé! Olé, Olé, Olé!' began: in his corner, like a Christian in the Coliseum, Jailauov could only look on in awe. He was a mere bit-part player in the night's proceedings. Dunne was pure theatre, arrogance and flair, and had the skill to match. He was the top dog in his own city, and he and the crowd knew it. The introductions were made, and the seconds retired, as the bell sounded to mark the beginning of Dunne's first defence of his European title.

Boxing is all about skill, power and psychology. As the boxers went about their job, Dunne had all three attributes in abundance, while Jailauov exuded an air of defeat in his very stance. His guard was low, and Dunne soon began to connect with his long jab, as he warmed to his task. Soon Dunne's right hand began to dictate proceedings, as left hooks to the body and head rained in on the challenger. As they went back to their corners at the end of the round, Dunne had the fight in his pocket. It was just a matter of time.

In the second, Dunne again came at his opponent with hooks and crosses, jabs and uppercuts. Various combinations bamboozled the impotent Jailauov, and the end of the fight seemed imminent. Jimmy Magee, RTÉ's doyen of the microphone, knew that the writing was on the wall for the challenger as he commented: 'If this goes the distance, Jailauov should patent the idea of longevity.'

The end of the fight was indeed at hand as the bell sounded at the start of the third round. Jailauov was facing the same fate he had suffered in his previous title attempt at the hands of Michael Hunter. His tank was empty – although, in truth, he had had nothing in it to begin with. Again, Bernard's jab dictated matters, and he followed up with an uppercut to the chin of his opponent. Thereafter, lefts and rights rained in at speed, as the referee Giuseppe Quartarone's patience wore thin. And then, Jailauov was dropped to the floor in what was deemed to be a slip. On the restart, Dunne connected with a sweet left to the body. The referee felt that it was low. Regardless, the fight was in its final stages as Dunne connected with an uppercut to floor Jailauov – and this time it was no slip. A count of eight only prolonged the farce and, following a further crisp right hand, the referee stepped in to lead the challenger back to his corner. It was over and, as expected, Dunne had been victorious in an all-too-easy manner. It had been a mismatch, and Dunne had never broken a sweat. For the neutral observer, there had been an obvious gulf in class, and the fight had been a poor spectacle. Still, it was fought twenty-three, won twenty-three for Dunne. Another full house would be assured at the Point Depot as long as the belt remained with the Dubliner.

Within the media, two distinct schools of thought were evident in the aftermath of Dunne's destruction of Jailauov. The first viewpoint was that Dunne had proved that he was too good for the European scene and would be better served by relinquishing that title and seeking world glory. However, there was a widely held belief in some quarters that Dunne had been involved in a complete mismatch. In the background, the name of Spain's Kiko Martinez was being mooted as the next viable opponent for the champion, but, as ever, Dunne's management would not be rushed. Speaking afterwards, trainer Harry Hawkins was keen to point out that the Martinez camp would accuse Dunne of running scared if he vacated the European title. Patience and caution were to be the watchwords of Dunne's career for the foreseeable future. Brian Peters often pointed to the fact that, after Barry McGuigan had won the European featherweight crown in 1983, it took him a further eight fights before he claimed the world title. The spectre of Kiko Martinez was beginning to haunt the career of Bernard Dunne: that bridge would be crossed at a later date.

As the summer of 2007 approached, the roof was due, literally, to come off the Point Depot in Dublin. The renovation work had been long overdue, and the imminent closure of the venue posed a dilemma to Bernard Dunne and his team, in that an alternative venue would need to be found to stage his title defences. The famous King's Hall in Belfast was one option on the horizon for Dunne, such was his appeal throughout Ireland.

However, the time was deemed right to place his belt on the line in late June; into the fray came an old adversary from Norway.

Reidar Walstad, who was ranked number three in Europe, had plenty of reasons to feel confident when he was named as Dunne's next challenger, in a fight to take place on 23 June. The main reason for this was that he had beaten Dunne in the European Amateur Championship in 1998. Dunne had indeed been on the wrong end of a result against Walstad in Belarus that year in a games at which Brian Magee had won a silver for Ireland in the middleweight class. Under the watchful eye of Harry Hawkins, seventeen-year-old Dunne, who was the then Irish junior and senior bantamweight champion, lost out on a 9–2 scoreline to the more experienced Norwegian, who would go on to claim a bronze medal at the games in the 54 kilogramme class. Nine years later, Walstad was keen to rekindle the memories of his victory as the prospect of a crack at Dunne's title became a reality. Having inflicted one of Dunne's few defeats during his amateur career, Walstad said that his 'confidence was high' and that a crack at the world title was his true aim.

As an amateur, Walstad had a record of note. He turned professional in January 2002 and was undefeated in his first nine paid contests. In February 2004, on the undercard of the Joe Calzaghe v. Mger Mkrtchyan WBO super-middleweight title fight, the Norwegian was stopped in the first round of his contest by Carlisle's Mongolia-born Shinny Bayaar at the Cardiff Arena. The short, sharp manner of Walstad's defeat that evening was a humiliating experience for the Norwegian, as his career seemed to be in tatters. However, he recovered from the setback to carve a respectable niche in the ranks by winning his next eight contests and securing his place in the ring with Dunne. Nevertheless, it was evident that the man who had beaten Dunne in 1998 had not progressed to the extent that the champion had since then. Talk of that previous meeting may have been irrelevant, but Walstad was keen to bring it up at every opportunity, saying: 'I know that we are both professionals now but for me Bernard still fights the same way as he did back then. I've watched a lot of his fights and I don't see much difference. He still makes the same mistakes and I will take advantage of those.'

Dunne was keen not to dwell on the past and, with an appropriate attack of amnesia, told the media that he didn't 'remember too much about their first meeting and was only concerned with the result on 23 June'. He added that the fight was 'a long time ago and I actually don't remember that much about the fight to be honest'. Dunne insisted, though, that the fight was in no way a revenge mission for him: 'It's not about revenge at all, I certainly don't look at it like that, and that first fight was all a long time ago, and what I need to do now is focus on the job at hand, just like I would for any other fight.'

The papers as usual hyped the contest to fever pitch and the Point Depot sold out in record time. The 'Viking Raider' was coming to Dublin to take Bernard's crown, and the city was not in the mood to tolerate such insolence again. Walstad was taking the challenge very seriously; he set up his training camp in London with a plethora of sparring talent brought in to assist in his preparations. He was skilful, determined and confident as the day of reckoning approached. At the weigh-in for the fight, the Norwegian eyed up Dunne's belt and declared to the media that he 'wanted that belt more than anything, even a world title'. He tipped the scales at half a pound under the 122-pound limit, while Dunne was spot on the weight. Despite his credentials, the Dublin bookmakers knew that a Walstad victory was a long shot, with odds of 12–1 quoted, while odds on Dunne were not quoted. The key to these odds was the fact that, given that Walstad had suffered only one defeat as a professional, his experience at the higher levels could not match Dunne's pedigree. As Benjamin Disraeli famously said: 'There are lies, damned lies and statistics.' But despite the fact that he had only one loss in sixteen outings, the vital statistic for Walstad was that he was taking a serious step up in class by fighting Dunne.

In the *Irish Times*, media writer Mary Hannigan described Walstad as looking 'as menacing as a choirboy'. With only hours to go before the action began, the Norwegian was still talking a good fight, however. On the vociferous Dublin supporters, Walstad was confident that he could handle the massive crowd who would be cheering for Dunne in the arena: 'Of course, it is only natural [that there is such strong support for Dunne], it is his hometown, but I'm sure I can win a decision this time. The judges always vote for the hometown guy so I know that I need to win it inside the distance and I believe I can do that.'

Dunne was pragmatic in his approach, telling the *News of the World* that he was relaxing before the fight by playing with his PlayStation, or playing cards with his trainer. But he was confident. He knew that he was the champion and that it would take a gargantuan effort from Walstad to take his belt. Looking beyond the fight, with a fleeting reference to the haunting spectre of Kiko Martinez, he added: 'He seems confident enough, and he'll certainly need it, stepping out in front of that crowd. I am sure it means that he's going to come out and have a real go. He's aggressive and has a lot of class, but I'm not too bad myself. I need to deal with Walstad first, obviously, but my next fight will probably be a mandatory defence against Kiko Martinez.'

But that clash was on the long finger as Bernard Dunne again took his place in the ring at the Point Depot on 23 June. The crowd roared as the dry ice filled the arena and, when the first notes of 'The Irish Rover' sounded, it was the Irish version of 'showtime' as well as party time in Dublin. The anthem was sung with gusto, the introductions were made and, nine years after the most famous victory of his career, Reidar Walstad was facing the champion of Europe, and the odds were stacked against him.

As the fight began, it was the left hooks and jabs of Dunne that set the early pace. In the second round, he let loose on his opponent, opening a serious cut above the Norwegian's left eye that told the tale of Dunne's punching power. This was merely the opening onslaught in a fight that Dunne had effectively wrapped up by the fourth round. The challenger was a durable customer who bravely stood and exchanged blows, exposing Dunne's apparent inability to finish an opponent off early. As the fight progressed, Dunne, while never in danger, became weary as his opponent's stubborn defence proved to be insurmountable. Dunne failed to punish the Norwegian, who smiled at him in defiance from the centre of the ring as the midway point came: despite the bravado, it was a sure sign that Walstad was in trouble.

As the fight wore on, the cut on Walstad's head deepened with every blow that Dunne landed. The Norwegian, despite the ferocious onslaught of Dunne, fought on gamely but the Dubliner was in total control and kept his opponent's challenge at a distance. An audible clash of heads prompted referee Luigi Muratore to call the doctor to the ring to examine the worsening condition of Walstad's eye; he was declared fit to box on. He was, however, a proverbial mile behind Dunne and, as the fight went into its closing stages, the champion eased home. The final bell saw Dunne climb the ropes – to the acclaim of the fans, who had witnessed another excellent display by their hero. He won by a unanimous decision, with the judges scoring it 118–111, 116–112 and 115–113 in favour of the champion. Sportingly, the Dublin crowd afforded Walstad a marvellous ovation for his valiant attempt to take the title. For Dunne, it was fought twenty-five, won twenty-five, and the good times continued.

With the second defence done and dusted, the inevitable question of Dunne's next opponent filled the pages of the local sports papers. With trainer Harry Hawkins insisting that a crack at the world title was still not on the agenda, a further defence of the European crown was considered the best option. The mandatory challenger was, of course, Kiko Martinez, and his name was duly put forward by the European Boxing Union; Martinez would have to be faced. Yet again, the Dunne hype was going into overdrive as, for the first time since 1972, when Muhammad Ali had defended his world crown against Al 'Blue' Lewis, Croke Park was again mooted as a possible venue for the fight. The Dunne phenomenon was again on a roll, with RTÉ reporting that the Walstad bout had attracted a peak audience of 607,000 viewers – 60 percent of the viewing audience. Rumours abounded that Sky Television and Setanta were about to bid to secure the rights for Dunne's defence of his title to Martinez, such was Dunne's attraction. As it turned out, Brian Peters won the bidding war, and the fight with Martinez was secured for the Point Depot on Saturday 25 August. RTÉ were again to show the fight live on terrestrial television.

The preparations began. Both Peters and Dunne knew that Martinez would be a serious step up in class, but the champion was certain that he had the ability to overcome the clunking fists of the Spaniard: 'Everyone is talking about Martinez because he has thirteen knock-outs from sixteen wins, so that's the kind of challenge that appeals to me . . . . He has a great record and he's been doing some talking but he's about to get his chance, and let's see what happens when somebody gets a chance to hit him back.' The contracts were signed and the tickets, as usual, were snapped up. However, defence number three was to provide Dunne with a completely different experience. Boxing can be a cruel sport, as Dunne was to learn.

10

BAD DAY AT THE POINT DEPOT

No one knows what to say in the loser's locker room.
Muhammad Ali

Kiko Martinez was nobody's fool, and had been stalking Dunne like a ghost for almost two years. As an amateur, he had had hopes of representing Spain at the Olympic Games and was undefeated in a vest, having knocked out thirty-eight of his forty opponents. After turning professional at eighteen, he came to the ring undefeated after sixteen fights, twelve of which had ended in knockouts within three rounds. Only once in his career had he gone twelve rounds, and that had been in April 2006, when he had defeated Frenchman John Bikai for the European Union belt. He had, by sheer power and determination, fought his way into the reckoning for Dunne's title. He stood only five feet four inches, but he had an effective crouching style and a dangerous punch.

At a press conference held on 16 July to publicise the

fight, the Spaniard was upbeat and showed no fear of the task ahead: 'This is the fight I've wanted for a long time. I might be a little shorter than Bernard but I'm five foot four inches of a headache for him. I have never lost a fight. I had forty amateur fights and was never beaten and I won thirty-eight of those by knockout. I could have gone to the Olympics, as the Spanish amateur boxing association wanted me to sign a four-year contract, but I wanted to turn professional. I'm looking forward to fighting in Dublin. I have boxed in front of big crowds before and I like to fight under pressure. Bernard is a good champion but I don't think he has boxed anyone like me and I am confident that I can win.'

Despite Martinez's reputation as a fierce puncher, Dunne was confident as the fight approached. Speaking at the same press conference, Dunne said, 'Kiko has a big reputation and is supposed to be a bit of a puncher, but I'm the champion and he's coming to my town so I'll let him worry about me. He's coming outside of Spain for the first time and he's never fought anyone in my class, so let's see what happens when someone starts hitting him back. I'll be looking to let my class and technical ability show, but if it turns into a fight then that suits me too because I love to get down in the trenches. My coach Harry Hawkins would prefer if I used my boxing ability and kept my distance, but sometimes you have to get up close and personal.'

The last line about getting 'up close and personal' would prove to be a prophetic statement. The last thing that Dunne wanted to do in the ring with Martinez was to get 'up close and personal'. Despite the fighting talk, there was nothing beyond the clunking fists of Martinez that suggested that he might trouble the champion. Most observers felt that the step up in class would prove to be too much for the Spaniard, and that Bernard Dunne's fighting style, along with the crowd and the occasion, would overwhelm him. As the day of the fight approached, all was well in the Dunne camp. The bout with Martinez was to be another forward step in securing Dunne a crack at the world title in 2008; defeat was unthinkable. Speaking at the Holy Trinity Gym in Belfast in the week before the fight, Dunne was playing the confidence card in the battle of words before the bout: 'Martinez is a big puncher, but so am I. Let's see what happens when somebody starts hitting him back. Look at his record; he's fought nobody in my class. I can tell you he's in for a big shock.'

For all the quotable remarks, Dunne knew that the big talking would only be done in the ring, at the packed arena. He and his entourage knew well the dangers that lay ahead, and Dunne had sparred hundreds of rounds in anticipation of Martinez's aggressive style. What lay at stake was the very future of Dunne's career; there could be no room for complacency. Many champions have lived to regret two of the most dangerous words in professional boxing: mandatory challenger.

The bill for the Dunne/Martinez clash was groundbreaking in more ways than one. For the first time ever, a British title fight would take place in the Republic of Ireland, with Belfast's Brian Magee fighting Tony Oakey for his British light-heavyweight title. Oakey was dismissive of the Belfast man in the run-up to the fight saying: 'It's going to take a special, special fighter to take it from me, and no disrespect but Brian Magee isn't that fighter. It doesn't matter if the fight is in Dublin or our back gardens.'

The fight was a classic, and Oakey retained his British crown with a majority draw decision, which did not go down well with the vociferous Dublin crowd. Two of the judges scored the fight a draw, while the third gave the decision to Magee. The crowd booed the decision but Magee had yet again been dealt an unlucky hand by the judges.

Better news for the Irish contingent came with the home debut of 2002 Olympian Andy Lee. The Limerick man, who had enjoyed a ten-fight unbeaten record outside Ireland, took on Belfast's Ciaran Healy in front of the large crowd. Lee, who had progressed greatly under the legendary American trainer Emanuel Steward, stormed his way to victory with a display of power-punching at the end of the fourth round. The Belfast man was retired by his seconds and remained on his stool at the beginning of the fifth; it had been an impressive homecoming for Lee.

Then came the moment of truth, as the arena awaited its very own Irish gladiator. The tension began to grow as television screens across Ireland were tuned in to what was meant to be the next instalment of the relentless climb through the ranks by Bernard Dunne. Kiko Martinez was announced into the arena and made his way to the ring through polite applause and, sadly, some booing, though a small group of supporters in the crowd brandished the Spanish flag. However, Kiko looked focused as he limbered up in the ring. A man dressed in Spanish national costume stood in the corner of the ring gesticulating to the crowd. Apart from that, there was no fuss as Kiko awaited the champion. RTÉ commentator Jimmy Magee summed up Kiko's predicament as he stood alone in the ring, surrounded by eight thousand passionate supporters of Dunne: 'A boxer will tell you that when you're in the ring, it makes no difference who's shouting, who's calling, and who's calling whom. But you cannot but be affected by this.'

Mike Goodhall, the master of ceremonies, awaited the confirmation that Dunne was ready and lifted the microphone to his lips to begin. Within seconds, the arena stood as one to greet 'Your very own champion, Dublin's Number One Son – Bernard Dunne.' The stage show, as always, was heightened as 'O Fortuna' by Carl Orf began in earnest. To everyone in the Point Depot, that piece was known simply as the theme tune to *The Omen* or, indeed, the music from the Old Spice advert from the 1970s. After a short delay, Dunne appeared through the dry ice into the brilliant light, and the crowd erupted. In the ring, Martinez kept to his warm-up routine as the dramatic music stopped suddenly, to be immediately followed by the feisty air of 'The Irish Rover'. The party was now in full swing as Bernard made his way to the ring. The cheers and applause reached a crescendo as the Dunne entourage climbed through the ropes, and it was a case of no turning back. As ever, there was complete respect for the opponent's anthem, while 'Amhrán na bhFiann' was belted out with gusto.

The introductions were made by Goodhall. Dunne looked composed and toned in his black shorts with a gold trim. Harry Hawkins went through the final instructions for his protégé, showing him how he wanted him to throw a right hand in the process. Promoter Brian Peters clapped his hands over his head to encourage the crowd and, accordingly, the noise in the arena reached fever pitch. Referee Terry O'Connor then called the two gladiators to the centre of the ring to remind them of the finer points of the Queensberry Rules, but their minds were miles away.

The two boxers return to their corners. Harry Hawkins gently slaps Dunne on the chin, reminding him of the plan: don't get caught cold. The chant of 'Olé! Olé, Olé, Olé!' reverberates around the hall as the bell goes to signal the start of round one: the crowd and Bernard Dunne are on the threshold of a truly shocking minute and a half of boxing.

Jimmy Magee and Dave 'Boy' McAuley take up their microphones and describe the action from ringside. Magee begins by describing the fight as 'another chapter in the great story of Bernard Dunne'. Immediately,

Martinez crouches low in the centre of the ring like a coiled spring, his left arm resting below his chin while his right arm hangs ominously below it. Dunne towers over his opponent, trying to work out his unusual style. Magee notes the peculiar stance of Martinez. Dunne feints and jabs while his opponent remains calm, waiting for his chance. Twenty seconds into the fight, Bernard attacks with a combination; the crowd react as Kiko throws a left and tries to connect with a right hand. McAuley at ringside comments on the Spaniard: 'he's like a miniature Mike Tyson, black boots and a similar style'. It is a prophetic statement: before he has finished speaking, Martinez opens up with a crisp right hand and follows up with a further thumping right that catches Dunne clean on the chin – and over he goes, as the crowd gasps as one. It is now a case of survival for Dunne, with only nineteen seconds having elapsed.

Dunne is on his feet immediately. He stares at the referee as he begins his count. He is hurt but not showing it, as he indicates he is fine. The count continues and Dunne points out to the referee that he slipped. He hadn't: his pride has been hurt in front of a disbelieving public. The nightmare scenario has happened: Dunne has been caught cold by a big hitter. The corner men are shouting at him to stay calm, keep to the plan. Martinez watches and waits from his own corner. The referee stares hard into Dunne's eyes; Dunne stares back at him. The crowd erupts and roars encouragement for Dunne as the referee tells him to keep his hands up and box on.

Jimmy Magee continues with his commentary: 'What a sensation within thirty-five seconds'. 'La Sensación' is living up to his name.

Martinez lines up his man and goes in for the kill. Dunne is now fighting on wits and instinct. Calmness is called for as his career stands on the edge of the abyss. Fifty-six seconds have now gone, as the arena screams encouragement for the Dubliner. However, he is in a corner, and the clunking fists are searching for him. 'Martinez is going after him,' says Magee. A haymaker over the top of Dunne's guard lands on the left side of his head, and he is down on the canvas for the second time within a minute. This was no slip, and the crowd can sense disaster. Dunne gets up like a drunken man looking for help. He tries to look into the eyes of the referee but he is unsteady, and the gasps in the arena are mixed with hopeless cries of encouragement. Dunne tries to convince Terry O'Connor that he is fine, but he has been hurt. In the corner, Harry Hawkins and Brian Peters stare through the madness at Dunne. Hawkins then glances at the referee and also at Martinez before staring back at Dunne. He has his towel at the ready.

The referee tells the protagonists to 'box on'. They go to the centre of the ring, where Dunne looks like a rabbit caught in headlights. The bell – and respite – is a hundred seconds away: too far to save him. Martinez knows what he is doing; he crouches and waits for his chance. A moment later, he opens up with a brutal combination: body shots and then a left hand to Dunne's head. He is a man on a mission, and can almost taste a sweet victory. 'If Dunne gets out of this, he is a great fighter,' says Magee into his microphone. 'He has to move, or he's going to get hurt,' adds McAuley. No sooner has he finished than Martinez catches Dunne with four punches to the head and Dunne is down again, distressed and, this time, out. Terry O'Connor has seen enough and waves his hands in the air. It is all over, and the ring is in pandemonium. The wild celebrations begin in the Spaniard's corner, while Harry Hawkins hugs and consoles the beaten Dunne. The crowd momentarily stands stunned, and many proceed to the exits.

The drama that unfolded that night shocked Ireland's sporting fraternity from the crown of its head to the tips of its bootstraps. Dunne's mandatory defence of his European super-bantamweight title against the man billed as 'La Sensación' lasted just eighty-six seconds. It was a cruel wake-up call, as Kiko Martinez clubbed his way through the champion's open guard and brutally exposed his defensive shortcomings. The collective party in the arena was stopped in its tracks, as silence and disbelief became the order of the day. The champion had lost, and lost badly. The Point, a former bus depot, had been due to close for major structural refurbishment in the week after the Dunne v. Martinez fight. As the 'Dublin Dynamo' lay battered on the canvas that evening, he could have been forgiven for believing that the walls of the old arena had come down around him in the first round. Dunne's career looked to be in crisis, as eight thousand fans streamed out of the arena wondering whether it had all been a dream, and whether they would ever see their hero fight at such a level again.

Muhammad Ali once said that the hardest place to be in the aftermath of a defeat is the loser's dressing room. For Dunne, the reality of the aftermath of defeat was to be played out live on the TV screens of Ireland. The true pain of the dressing room would have to wait. It was a truly shattering experience for the Dublin man, whose career, it seemed, lay in tatters. The shock, and the suddenness of the loss, would not sink in immediately, as he had to compose himself enough to address the media and the crowd from the ring: it was all part of the television buy-in. Dunne, however, held it together, and sportingly paid tribute to Martinez. He thanked his supporters and said that he would have to go back to the drawing board to resurrect his career. He was hurting badly but the pain would only come out properly in the privacy of the dressing room. The fight that had been meant to launch Dunne on to the world stage had ended in utter humiliation. The world-title shot was now a pipe dream, and it was a case of thinking hard about the future. One thing was for certain, however, and that was that the party was most definitely over for the time being. Any notions of filling the Point Depot in the foreseeable future were dashed. The talking between manager, trainer, promoter and boxer would be long and hard.

At the post-fight press conference, the rumour mill was red-hot. There were stories that Kiko's entourage had placed a massive sum of money, at odds of 66–1, that their man would stop the fight in the first round. They had pulled off the betting coup of the year in Dublin. The talk now was of a world-title shot for Martinez, not Dunne. When he spoke, Bernard was again gracious in defeat and philosophical about what had happened. He admitted that he had been caught cold and agreed that he would have to undergo a period of reflection: 'I will take it little by little. I need more experience, and then I will hopefully fight for a world title. I got hit with a punch that I didn't see coming and from there I was in trouble. I'm just so disappointed for myself and everyone in the team and I feel that I have let the people down. The support they showed me at the start and after the fight was tremendous. The Irish fans are just fantastic. Now I have to go away from this and watch the tape and see where I went wrong. It's hard to take, but that's boxing. I know that I have the character to come back from this and I'll prove that. I can come back even stronger.'

The talk was also of a rematch between Dunne and Martinez. Not surprisingly, the Spaniards indicated that they would be happy to return to Ireland. That prospect was something that the Dunne camp would not countenance in the short-term. It was going to take a more circuitous route to get Dunne back in the reckoning. He had not been outboxed by Martinez, nor had he been worn down by the Spaniard. He had quite simply been caught cold by Martinez's clunking fists. He was the not the first champion to suffer such a fate, nor would he be the last. However, as morning broke on Sunday 26 August, Bernard Dunne's dreams lay in tatters. He had to think long and hard and put the defeat in perspective. Never a man to hide away from the world, Dunne, like thousands of other proud Dubliners, headed to Croke Park to see the Dubs take on Kerry in the All-Ireland football semi-final. There was no point in Bernard feeling sorry for himself – a world title was still a possibility. All that was needed was hard work, determination and, of course, a little bit of luck. Yet again, Bernard Dunne was being asked if he had 'bounce-back-ability'.

11

A GHOST IN THE HOUSE

'What he needs to do now is answer that tough but honest question himself: "Do I still have what it takes to succeed?"'

Sugar Ray Leonard on Bernard Dunne

Sometimes in sport, words said in haste can come back to haunt an individual. Prior to the clash with Kiko Martinez, Bernard Dunne had told RTÉ: 'I won't be standing in front of him letting him hit me – I'll be moving all the time, making him work and keeping him under pressure, keeping him thinking.' In retrospect, Dunne's game plan went very wrong on the night. Learning from one's mistakes is all part of life, but coming back from a defeat as devastating as the one inflicted by Martinez was going to take a massive effort. Dunne was going to have to prove himself in the face of serious adversity. The period of reflection was going to be long and hard as 'Plan B' was formulated.

In June 1986, when world champion Barry McGuigan was knocked out by Steve Cruz in the blistering Las Vegas heat, the setback was to signal the waning of a glorious career. The defeat was followed by recriminations, and a festering resentment between manager, trainer and boxer that would eventually end up in the Belfast High Court. The devastating defeat by Cruz had a far-reaching effect on McGuigan. For both Wayne McCullough and Steve Collins, the greatest setbacks of their careers came via anomalies discovered in routine brain scans. For Collins, the news of the irregularity effectively ended his career in the ring; for McCullough, a long, painful and protracted battle was waged to get himself a clean bill of health. Bernard Dunne had experienced the low of having his career put in jeopardy by an irregular brain scan and had come back to the sport a stronger individual after having been given the all-clear. Defeat was a different matter, and the manner in which it was inflicted had been painful. It was now a test of character for the twenty-seven-year-old Dubliner. The unparalleled appeal of Dunne at the box office had vanished in the space of eighty-six seconds, while the road to the top became, yet again, a long and arduous one. The spectre of Kiko Martinez had haunted Dunne before the two had clashed, and it was now time that his memory was exorcised.

While Dunne and his team plotted a comeback for the former champion, Martinez was to return to Ireland in double-quick time when it was announced that he was to fight Wayne McCullough at Belfast's King's Hall in

December. The fight was the latest in the series of 'comeback' bouts that the thirty-seven-year-old McCullough had secured, but as he had not fought for two years, the EBU refused to sanction the bout. McCullough's recent inactivity meant that there was to be no title at stake, and therefore the fight was a glorified challenge contest.

At the time of the scheduled fight, Wayne McCullough was many years past his best. At stake was a point of principle, though. If McCullough could put up a fighting performance against the Spaniard – or even beat him – it would be a massive boost to his flagging career and would put him in the reckoning for a title shot. For a man who had not fought in Belfast in five years, McCullough knew that the fight with Martinez presented him with an opportunity which was too good to miss: 'I can't wait to fight in front of my home fans. I'm really looking forward to it. I haven't fought in Belfast since 2002, and while I constantly asked for a fight over there, it just didn't happen. Even though I've lived in Las Vegas for the past fourteen years, I never forgot where I came from, and my fans have stood by me. I made the first defence of my WBC bantamweight belt back in 1995 in Belfast, and the support I got – and continue to get – from the fans over there is unbelievable. I'm really excited about this fight.'

McCullough, who had not fought since 2005, when he lost a WBC super-bantamweight title fight against Oscar Larios in Las Vegas, knew the importance of the fight with Martinez. What happened on the day of the weigh-in in Belfast was pure farce: the fight was cancelled when Martinez was one and three-quarter pounds over the agreed weight. In fact, the names of both McCullough and Martinez were to be sullied as chaos reigned at Belfast's King's Hall. The Spaniard was given an hour to 'sweat off' the excess weight but remained seated in the arena sipping from a bottle of water. Meanwhile, an unsightly war of words began between Wayne and his wife Cheryl on one side and the veteran *Belfast Telegraph* journalist Jack Magowan on the other. The bickering began when Magowan was heard to criticise McCullough over the fact that he had weighed in a full three pounds under the agreed limit – which was peculiar in itself. What followed was an angry exchange of words that did nothing for the image of the sport, given that it took place under the gaze of the assembled media. Martinez never returned to the scales; his team refused to fight McCullough at a new weight, and the bill was cancelled by the disgusted promoter Pat Magee. It had been an embarrassment, to say the least.

After a lay-off of eight months, Bernard Dunne's career finally creaked back into action on 12 April 2008, when he was matched with the former world champion Felix Machado from Venezuela at the International Events Arena in Castlebar, County Mayo. The Point Depot was out of commission and, in any case, Dunne would not fill such a high-profile venue after losing his title. A change of place and mindset was needed, and

Dunne hit the road again. The bill was labelled 'Into the West': it was the first time that international boxing of such a high calibre had taken place in County Mayo. A boxer out of action or 'picking up' time as Dunne had been doing, is not earning good money or gaining experience. Bernard Dunne's family life, however, compensated for the lack of fighting: in December, Pamela and Bernard celebrated the arrival of their second child, a son, Finian. In addition, Dunne finished his gruelling training with the Dublin Fire Brigade and qualified as a fireman – a fact that perhaps suggested that Dunne was thinking ahead in the event that his boxing career vanished overnight. It was a shrewd move for a man who had seen how fickle boxing can be.

Speaking to the press in the build-up to the contest, Dunne explained that the fight with Martinez had affected him badly and that he was eager for a rematch: 'From the moment I got out of the ring I've wanted another crack at Martinez, and that hasn't changed. I'd get back in there with him tomorrow if it was possible. We're both in different promotional camps so I don't know if the rematch can be made, but I certainly want it. I'm not obsessed with it. If the fight comes up, great, but if not, we have our own plan. But it's only natural that I'd want to settle the score.'

Brian Peters was realistic and pointed out that a crack at Martinez would be a longer-term project. The fact was, however, that any notions of greatness that Martinez had were dented in March 2008 when he lost his European belt to Rendall Munroe in Nottingham. The fight was close, and Munroe claimed it only by majority verdict after twelve gruelling rounds. For Dunne, the fact was that he probably would have outboxed Martinez comfortably if their fight had gone beyond three rounds. In boxing parlance, Martinez, with his big punch, was a 'one-trick pony', and this fact was now evident.

The bout with Machado would be the first obstacle in what was described as Dunne's 'rehabilitation' in boxing terms. One important decision which was taken by Brian Peters and Harry Hawkins in respect of Dunne was hiring the services of Mike McGurn, an expert physical trainer. McGurn's pedigree in being able to get results with athletes had been shown when he had taken a role in 2002 with the Irish rugby set-up; his involvement had reaped an immediate reward for the international team as Triple Crown victories in 2004, 2006 and 2007. To help Dunne climb back to the top of the rankings would require an added dimension; McGurn was considered to be the man to do just that. The aim was to add bulk to Dunne's physique in order to add the power that would see him compete again with the best in the world.

There was no doubting that Machado was a class act. However, at thirty-five years old, it was undeniable that he was past his best in terms of his boxing ability. His career as a professional began in 1993, when he was defeated in his native Venezuela by Jesus Rattia. He recovered from that reversal to go on to claim the national title, and in 2000 he fought out a draw against Julio Gamboa for the vacant IBF super-flyweight title. In the rematch five months later, Machado made no mistakes and took the title; he defended it on three occasions before losing it to Luis Alberto Perez in January 2004. After being defeated by Perez again in the subsequent rematch, Machado's career went into decline; going into the fight with Dunne, he had lost his five previous contests. On paper, Machado was a perfect opponent for Dunne after the defeat to Martinez.

Regardless, the pressure was on Dunne, who was seen in many circles as 'damaged goods'. The fact was that Machado was a boxer on the way to retirement, and not a contender for any title. This added to a degree of scepticism surrounding the fight. However, the real fight for Bernard Dunne was psychological; he had the boxing ability to win, but he had to address the issue of whether the defeat to Martinez had affected his mind and confidence. As it was, the Breaffy House Hotel venue had the 'full house' signs posted on the night of the bill: the fans still believed in Dunne.

On the night itself, RTÉ also showed their faith in Dunne by screening the fight live. The crowds turned out, and Dunne ended his eight-month sojourn by claiming a points victory. The final score, according to the referee Emile Tiedt, was 100–90 to Dunne, which indicated that he had won each round. The most important aspect, though, was that Dunne had made and survived the comeback, despite a touch of apparent ring rustiness. Bernard opened the fight in fine form and made some solid shots to the head and body of the southpaw. In the fifth, after being the victim of a couple of low blows, Dunne's right eye was opened by Machado, causing a minor headache for his corner men. As the fight entered its last three rounds, there was a sense within the arena that Dunne was as good as home and that Machado had nothing left to trouble the Dubliner. Refusing to retreat, Dunne opened-up on his opponent by firing excellent combinations to finish with a flourish and, in the end, was a worthy winner. His record was now fought twenty-six, won twenty-five and lost one.

Speaking to Marty Morrissey of RTÉ afterwards, Dunne explained that the Venezuelan had been a tough opponent throughout: 'We expected Felix to come out and test me, and he did. I'm a bit disappointed, I threw a good right to the body in the second round but wasn't able to follow up on it. Overall, I thought I did well enough. He's a seasoned campaigner. I'd like to thank him very much for coming over and giving me the chance to fight him. To be honest, I was anxious about coming back in. Also, although this is my home soil, fighting in Mayo was new to me too, but the crowd gave me great support. I didn't box great, I should have been quicker, my hands weren't great, but to win the fight without boxing well tells you all you need to know.'

Within a month, Brian Peters announced that the next stage of Bernard Dunne's comeback would take place in the National Stadium in Dublin on 12 July. Peters had hoped to get an earlier date for Dunne but the problems associated with the hand and eye injuries that he had picked up in the fight with Machado had meant that more recuperation time was required. The arena on the South Circular Road was, of course, a smaller venue than the Point Depot, but it was a second homecoming for Dunne. While no opponent was announced for Dunne, the fact was that the reigning European super-bantamweight champion, Rendall Munroe, was under contract with Sky Sports, and thus his choice of opponents had been arranged somewhat in advance. However, when you have scaled the heights to become European champion, you have little more to prove at this level, particularly once you have defended the title. The prospect of chasing Munroe was unappealing to Dunne, and his goals were re-assessed. Also out of the equation was a rematch with Martinez, given that there was no value in such a bout since the Spaniard had lost his title; such a fight would be pure madness for Dunne.

As it was, Argentinian Damian Marchiano was chosen to be Dunne's opponent at the National Stadium. The twenty-eight-year-old did not have a pedigree to match that of Machado, having turned professional only in 2001, but he was still considered to be dangerous. He had won the South American bantamweight crown in 2004 and, thereafter, had moved to the United States in search of further glory. At the end of May, he had lost by a fifth-round knockout to Silence Mabuza in Atlantic City in a clash for the IBO bantamweight title. By agreeing to go in against Dunne within six weeks of that defeat, there was a suspicion that he was acting somewhat hastily on the rebound from that defeat. However, Dunne badly needed to win the fight if he was to re-establish himself as a credible challenger. The clamour for tickets was less than overwhelming, though: reports suggested that it would be a struggle to fill the two-thousand-seater arena for Dunne's fight with the Argentinian.

One person who still followed the career of Dunne with great interest was Sugar Ray Leonard. Sugar Ray questioned Dunne's state of mind, especially in light of the fact that he had recently qualified as a fireman. Speaking to *ESPN.com*, Leonard questioned whether Dunne wanted to be 'Fighter of the Year' or 'Fireman of the Year'. He added: 'From the very first time I met and worked with Bernard Dunne, I saw incredible potential . . . Bernard has to do what is quite difficult for all fighters, including what yours truly had to do . . . . It depends on his health, mindset and desire – which nobody knows but Bernard himself. What he needs to do now is answer that tough but honest question himself . . . "Do I still have what it takes to succeed?"'

In the end, Dunne came through the fight with relative ease and, for the second time in seven weeks, he never lost a round during a fight. The crowd again turned out in force and the National Stadium had the 'house full' signs up as the loyal Dubliners cheered their hero home against an opponent who was stylish but failed to threaten the Neilstown man. Dunne boxed wisely and kept the fight at a distance rather than getting into the brawl that the Argentinian wanted. During the second round, Dunne went to the canvas – the result of a slip – but soon recaptured his composure. By the seventh, Dave 'Boy' McAuley, doing the commentary for RTÉ with Jimmy Magee, suggested that Dunne looked as 'fresh as paint', such was his dominance and fitness. At the end, the referee gave the bout to Dunne on a 100–90 scoreline, but the question remained in many minds as to what a boxer of Bernard Dunne's stature could possibly learn from such an exercise. It seemed that the cautious approach being adopted to get Bernard back into contention would need to run its course, however long that would take.

There was a perception in boxing circles that since his defeat to Martinez, Dunne was being shielded from the so-called 'big-hitters' of the super-bantamweight class. This notion was to be tested, however, when the name of Dunne's opponent was announced for his second trip to the Breaffy House Hotel in Castlebar on 15 November. With a record of sixteen wins – eleven by knockout – and three defeats in nineteen fights, Cristian Faccio from Uruguay also had a reputation as someone with an ability to throw a powerful punch. His stance and style were perceived to be somewhat crude, but there was no doubting that he packed power, and this was the type of challenge that Bernard Dunne relished – and needed. During his career, Faccio had been stopped twice and, given his tendency to leave himself open to a well-delivered punch, was no stranger to the canvas. To a skilled boxer of

Dunne's class, this test would provide him with an opponent similar to Kiko Martinez; if the Dubliner was to reach the top again, he was going to need this experience.

Originally, Mexico's Eduardo Garcia had been agreed on as Dunne's opponent. However, the hard-hitting former North American bantamweight champion had to withdraw from the fight due to a hand injury, and the search began for a replacement. Faccio was a perfect substitute. He was the reigning Latin American bantamweight champion and had, in June 2008, fought Japan's Hozumi Hasegawa for the WBC title in Tokyo. In that fight, the Uruguayan went for broke and was caught by the champion in the second with a sweet left which had him sprawling in the ring before the referee, wisely, stopped the fight. The prospect of taking on an opponent who had, five months previously, fought the WBC world champion would not do any harm to Dunne's credibility.

In reality, the defeat to Kiko Martinez had knocked Bernard Dunne's world-title plans back by at least eighteen months. The two wins since that defeat had gone a long way to convincing his trainer Harry Hawkins that his protégé was again ready to take his chance and fight for a world title. Speaking to David Kelly of the *Belfast Telegraph*, Hawkins indicated that the Martinez defeat had been, more or less, consigned to history: 'The old Bernard Dunne is back in the gym now and in his next fight he's going to face a top-ten fighter in the world, and that will give him the chance to answer all the questions.

What has pleased me is the way he has shown the mental strength to come back from such a defeat. I wouldn't have said that he was ready for a world title after his first fight back, but after the second one I could really see the confidence coming back. Now, with one more impressive win against someone in the top ten, he'll certainly be ready for any of the world champions.'

Faccio, however, was not coming to Mayo to make up the numbers. The twenty-five-year-old had fast hands and experience galore. He had fought for a world title and was out to prove his credentials as a contender once again. He believed that Dunne was susceptible to a hard punch and told the press that he would adopt the same tactic as had Martinez: he would be going out to land the big punch. Dunne, however, had learned from bitter experience and, surely, would not fall prey to an early 'haymaker'. The key to the clash would lie in Dunne's ability to avoid the big shots, use his undoubted boxing skill, and subdue his opponent. The fight certainly whetted the appetite of the expectant crowd in the arena that November evening. On live television, the Irish public tuned in in their tens of thousands to see whether Dunne could negotiate this latest hurdle. The anthem and 'Irish Rover' were sung with gusto, and the introductions were made in the packed hall: Bernard Dunne had it all to do against an opponent rated tenth in the WBC rankings.

The early rounds saw Dunne at his best. He was cautious, and dictated the contest at his own pace from the off. Faccio was eager to attack and came forward in search of the big punch, but Dunne was too shrewd and kept his opponent at bay. By the seventh round, Dunne had the fight in his pocket, as referee Emile Tiedt was heard to tell both protagonists to 'watch your heads'. Within seconds, a sickening clash of skulls was audible at ringside and, immediately, it was evident that Dunne had come off second-best. Blood began to gush from his forehead into his eyes, and from then it was only a matter of time before the fight was stopped. However, both men went for broke, with Faccio seizing the initiative and sensing that Dunne was in trouble. As the bell sounded for the end of the round, it was evident that Dunne would not be able to continue, and his corner called for the referee, to advise him of the situation. The blood would not stop flowing: that was that, as far as Dunne was concerned.

The fight was over, and it fell to the referee to call the fight as he saw it until that stage of the contest, as the clash had been purely accidental. (If a fight is stopped as a result of an accident, it goes to the scorecard of the referee.) Tiedt had Dunne ahead by 70–65; thus, Dunne had won every round. It was an unexpected and unhappy ending to the fight. In hurling terms, Dunne had been 'split'; as far as going into the ring was concerned, the prospect of an immediate world-title attempt would be severely delayed. The disappointment of the manner in which the fight had ended seemed to indicate that Dunne's luck had run out. However, in boxing, as in life, an unexpected opportunity can sometimes present itself at the most unexpected time. For Bernard Dunne, his life and career would be changed – and changed utterly – within four months of leaving the ring that November night. Despite the unhappy ending to the fight with Faccio, glory awaited in 2009.

12

THE MATCH IS MADE

Life is what happens to you while you're busy making other plans.

John Lennon

Christmas 2008 came early for Bernard Dunne, as the news broke on 24 December that his management team had secured for him a crack at the WBA champion, Ricardo Cordoba from Panama. More importantly, the fight would take place on 21 March in Dublin's re-christened O2 Arena, formerly The Point, the scene of 'that night' when he was humiliated by Kiko Martinez. This was the chance that Dunne had waited for; the chance to exorcise the ghost of Martinez in front of his own fans. His progress following the defeat to Martinez had been good, if unspectacular. Going in with the world champion was a step up in class for Dunne, but this was too good to be true. His star had been on the rise, and there had been persistent rumours of a clash with European champion Rendall Munroe. However, the intricacies of the negotiations between Brian Peters and Frank Maloney ended in deadlock, and the fight was put on the long finger. That deadlock was to work out in favour of Dunne as an opportunity of gargantuan proportions presented itself in the days leading up to Christmas: in essence, as one door closed, the chance of a lifetime came along through another.

The crack at Ricardo 'El Maestrito' Cordoba's WBA super-bantamweight crown came about by sheer luck. For Bernard Dunne, it was a case of being available at the right time and being prepared to take a chance. It was a calculated risk, but when the chance to take such a risk presents itself, a boxer must be prepared to take it with both hands. Dunne put the fight in perspective at the press conference to announce the fight: 'This is the fight I've wanted since I first put on a pair of boxing gloves. It's every boxer's dream to be a world champion, and I'm no different. This is what I've worked my whole life for, and now that the chance is here, I want to grab it with both hands. Every boxer wants to fight for a world title, but to have it in your hometown is special. It's going to be an incredible experience, and I know I'll thrive on that atmosphere. Cordoba's fought all around the world, but he won't ever have experienced anything like the atmosphere in the O2. It's going to be very special. It's a fantastic venue, and 21 March can't come soon enough.'

Brian Peters is a shrewd promoter. The rumour mill went into overdrive, and it was suggested that Peters had offered Cordoba €200,000 to defend his title against Dunne at the newly refurbished, 9,500 capacity O2 Arena. With Bernard Dunne's reputation still tarnished by the Martinez defeat, Peters was taking a gamble in that the public would need to be convinced that an upset was on the cards and, quite possibly, Dunne could beat Cordoba. Given that the Celtic Tiger was a distant memory and people's economic realities had changed, it was going to be an uphill battle to fill the venue. Peters has a tendency to trust his own intuition; he had deep faith in Dunne's ability and, as proof of this, was prepared to promote the fight. Also, Peters knew that a world-title fight in Dublin would capture the imagination of the home supporters and help Dunne make history on 21 March. He had followed Dunne from his days as an amateur and knew that, deep down, he would not be found wanting against the champion. Speaking at the initial press conference, Peters outlined his reasons for bringing the fight to Dublin and reiterated his absolute faith in Dunne's fighting ability: 'This is a huge event for Ireland, as world-title fights are often talked about but in reality they don't come along too often. I think this has all the makings of a historic night for Irish sport. From the first time I saw Bernard as an amateur, I believed he was destined to be a world champion. It's been a long road, but where better for that dream to become reality than at the fabulous new O2 in his hometown.'

Twenty-four-year-old Ricardo Cordoba was nicknamed 'El Maestrito', which translates as 'The Teacher'.

He certainly had an impressive pedigree. In September 2008, Cordoba had taken the interim WBA title when he unanimously outpointed Luis Perez in his native Panama City. Two months later, he was made the 'official' champion when his old rival Celestino Caballero claimed the IBF belt in a unification fight. For Cordoba, a clash with Caballero would wait, as he needed some defences under his world belt. That is where Bernard Dunne came into the equation.

In August 2005, Cordoba had been denied by the narrowest of split decisions in a previous attempt at the same title. That defeat was the only blemish in a thirty-seven-fight record that began at the age of fifteen in September 2000, when he knocked out Hussein Sanchez in the first round of their fight. A gifted amateur, he had been given the nickname 'The Teacher' as a twelve-year-old due to his ability to hand out boxing lessons to fighters much older than himself. He was invincible in his native Panama and had, significantly, beaten fellow Panamanian and IBF champion Celestino Caballero. When a proposed unification bout with Caberello vanished into the ether, it was Brian Peters who stepped in to ensure that Cordoba's first defence would be against Bernard Dunne. Dunne was ranked number eleven by the WBA; for Cordoba, the words 'routine defence' must have entered his head. Soon after the match was made, the Panamanian was somewhat flippant about Dunne's chances, telling *Boxing News*: 'I know his name and record, and I'm told that he's a good technical boxer, and that's all I need to know for now.'

As the date with destiny neared, Cordoba was more circumspect. He said he believed that the fight with Dunne was crucial in his quest to reach legendary status in the super-bantamweight division: 'I want to be world champion for a very long time and prove to the world that I am a great fighter, so I can't allow somebody like Bernard Dunne to get in my way.'

In sport, history has a habit of repeating itself: there had, of course, been a precedent for an Irishman challenging a Panamanian for a world title. Saturday 8 June 1985 was a humid evening at London's Loftus Road football ground, as twenty-seven thousand avid followers of Barry McGuigan made their way to see a truly epic encounter. The career of the 'Clones Cyclone' had been skilfully managed from his debut in Dublin in 1981, and four years later he went in as an underdog against the legendary WBA featherweight champion Eusebio Pedroza from Panama. Pedroza had held the title since 1978, defending it on a record nineteen occasions in the process. He was a hero in his native country and would eventually be inducted into boxing's International Hall of Fame.

The fight was an epic encounter – fifteen rounds of sheer excitement and exhilaration. Carried live on television throughout the UK and Ireland, the fight was sheer drama. McGuigan gave the fight of his life and, in the seventh round, hit the champion with the sweetest right hand, flooring him. Twice more, he had Pedroza floundering in the ring as the fight ebbed and flowed. In the end, the party to end all parties began as McGuigan was awarded a unanimous fifteen-round decision. The streets of Belfast, Clones and beyond celebrated in style, and the festivities lasted well into the following week. The victory has entered Irish sporting folklore and is up there with 'that Houghton goal' in 1988 against England, 'that O'Leary penalty at Italia '90' and, topically for 2009, 'that win in Cardiff'. In December that year, McGuigan was named BBC Sports Personality of the Year, becoming the first person not born in the United Kingdom to win the award. Could Irish sporting history repeat itself twenty-three years after 'that McGuigan fight'? Dare I add that in 1985, Irish rugby was on the crest of a wave, with the international side having won the Triple Crown? The similarities were too good to be true. The O2 Arena was primed and ready for drama.

Team Cordoba left Panama for Ireland on 10 March. The fact that he was going to fight Dunne in Dublin in front of a partisan crowd did not affect the champion's thinking. He said that he was prepared for the battle ahead and that his ultimate victory would be dedicated to his two sons, Ricardo and Maikol. Cordoba was determined and assured at the airport when he told reporters: 'I am leaving very motivated, with total faith in my victory, and sure that I will return to my country as a champion. I have seen his fights, there is no doubt he is good, but I have studied his style and I am going with an effective plan to neutralise him.

'The title is coming back to Panama with me because I am not going to give up this belt. I have worked too hard to become world champion to just throw it all away. I'm very confident and I feel in great shape. In fact, the last time I felt as good before a fight was when I beat Celestino Caballero back in 2004, so if that's anything to go by, Dunne is in a lot of trouble.'

After Dunne had secured the scalps of the three South Americans, he was ranked number eleven by the WBA. The training under Harry Hawkins had gone well in the Holy Trinity Club in Belfast's Turf Lodge district, and he described himself as 'ready' as the fight drew near. Significantly, Dunne had adopted a holistic approach to his preparations for the clash with Cordoba, having sought the services of the renowned strength-and-conditioning coach Mike McGurn. In addition, Dunne had adopted a radical approach to his diet and nutrition. In short, no stone was left unturned as he sought to reach his absolute peak. While he was quite a distance away from being a mandatory challenger, Dunne believed that this fact was irrelevant as the fight drew near: 'That's for the bookies to decide. That might take a bit of the pressure off me, but at the end of the day it will only be the two of us in the ring, and whether you're labelled the favourite or the underdog it doesn't matter as soon as you step between those ropes. It's what you do in that ring on the night that counts, and I know I'm as good as anyone else out there. If I didn't believe that, then I'd have no business [being] in there.'

Dunne was fully aware that Cordoba was vulnerable outside of his native Panama. The champion had fought on only three occasions outside his home country and had recorded two draws and one defeat; could there be a weakness that Dunne could exploit? He also understood how crucial it was to have a packed arena behind him, and believed that fighting in front of his home fans would inspire him to victory. 'Every boxer wants to fight for a world title, but to have [the contest] in your home-town is very special,' he said. 'It's going to be an incredible experience and I know I'll thrive on that atmosphere. Cordoba's fought all around the world but he won't ever have experienced anything like the atmosphere in the O2.'

The Dunne v. Cordoba fight, on 21 March, was to be a night to remember for Irish boxing. Brian Peters knew well that Irish boxing was on an all-time high after Ireland's treble medal winning Olympic heroics in Beijing, and the bill that evening was to include the cream of the amateur and professional ranks of the sport. The main attraction was to be the clash between Kenny Egan and China's Zhang Xiaoping, who had denied him the Olympic gold medal five months previously in Beijing. For Egan, this was his opportunity to avenge the 11–7 defeat in the final, which many neutrals, as well as the Irish, felt was unfair. A crowd of 9,500 would be in attendance to roar on the Irish captain, and it was a real coup for Brian Peters to secure the Olympic champion for the bill. At the press conference, Egan was relishing the prospect of a rematch: 'I'm keeping my fingers, toes and everything else crossed that he comes . . . It would show great sportsmanship on his part to come over and give me a rematch in Ireland. The last time I boxed him was in a huge venue full of Chinese people, so it would be nice to fight him in a huge venue over here full of Irish people this time.'

Paddy Barnes, the Belfast light-flyweight who claimed bronze at the Beijing Olympics, was soon added to the bill. In arranging the undercard, Peters acknowledged the growing appeal of women's boxing. If you want to put on a top-class bill, there is a fine exponent of the women's game who has brought glory to Ireland on a world stage. Born in 1986, Bray's Katie Taylor set Irish women's boxing on fire with some remarkable displays of skill and determination across the globe. At the 2006 World Amateur Championships in New Delhi, Taylor took the gold medal by defeating Anabella Farias of Argentina in the 60 kilogramme final. She followed this victory by retaining that title in 2008 when she defeated China's Cheng Dong in the final. She was given her opportunity to show her ability in front of the widest possible audience when she was matched with the Pan-American champion Caroline Barry of the United States on the undercard of the bill. It was the greatest boost possible for the fledgling sport, and the public were eager to see another Irish hero in action at the arena. Speaking at the press conference arranged to publicise the bill, Taylor, who had been awarded the accolade of Irish Sportswoman of the Year for 2008, expressed her excitement at the prospect of fighting on such a bill: 'This is a huge opportunity for me. It is really going to be a big night for Irish boxing and a great chance for me to perform on a big stage, so I'm looking forward to it.'

Limerick's Andy Lee, whose scheduled fight in Madison Square Garden, New York, had been cancelled at short notice, was a late addition to the card; he was matched with the German Alex Sipos. Lee was a perfect replacement for Kenny Egan, who was forced to withdraw for personal reasons. The bout involving Lee would be the main supporting bout to precede Dunne's crack at Cordoba. Making up the rest of the undercard would be Cavan's Andy Murray, who would be attempting to take Daniel Rasilla's EU lightweight title, while the ageless hero of the Dublin crowd, Jim 'Pink Panther' Rock, would face the Italian Alessio Furlan. It was all systems go for the biggest night that Dublin boxing had witnessed since Croke Park played host to Muhammad Ali in 1972.

As the fight neared, the ghost of Kiko Martinez must have haunted Dunne as he contemplated a return to the O2 Arena. The silence of defeat is truly deafening, and Dunne had heard it once before. However, Dunne was confident and 'buzzing' as he met the press in the National Stadium. The loss to Martinez had changed the perception that people held of Bernard Dunne. The prospect of the fight with Cordoba was viewed as a 'bridge too far' for Dunne by some, and the media expected a 'spirited performance', with the title being a long shot for the Dubliner. In order to believe that

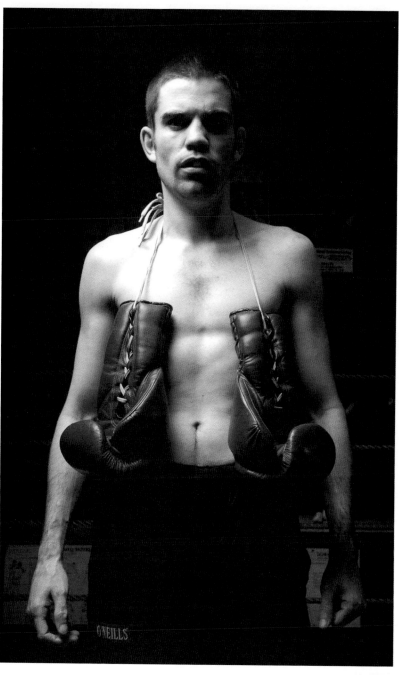

(SPORTSFILE)

Bernard Dunne with trainer Harry Hawkins, Holy Trinity Boxing Club, Belfast (Oliver McVeigh / SPORTSFILE)

Bernard Dunne celebrates with the Irish flag after defeating Esham Pickering to win the European super bantamweight title at the Point Depot, Dublin (Ray Lohan / SPORTSFILE)

WBA world super bantamweight title holder Ricardo 'El Maestrito' Cordoba arrives at a press conference on 29 January 2009 to announce details of his title defence against Bernard Dunne, on 21 March at the O2 Arena, Dublin (Stephen Mooney / SPORTSFILE)

Bernard Dunne in action against Ricardo Cordoba on 21 March 2009, during their WBA world super bantamweight title fight at the O2, Dublin (David Maher / SPORTSFILE)

Bernard Dunne puts Ricardo Cordoba down during the third round of their WBA world super bantamweight title fight (David Maher / SPORTSFILE)

Bernard Dunne celebrates with promoter Brian Peters, right, and trainer Harry Hawkins after knocking down Ricardo Cordoba in the eleventh round to win the WBA world super bantamweight title (David Maher / SPORTSFILE)

Boxing promoter Brian Peters, centre, with Bernard Dunne and WBA super bantamweight title holder Ricardo 'El Maestrito' Cordoba after a press conference at the O2
Arena, Dublin, on 29 January 2009 (Brian Lawless / SPORTSFILE)

Bernard Dunne, left, and Kiko Martinez at the weigh-in and press conference at the
Burlington Hotel, Dublin, on 24 August 2007 (David Maher / SPORTSFILE)

Kiko Martinez lands a left on Bernard Dunne during the first round of their European super bantamweight title fight at the Point Depot, Dublin, on 25 August 2007 (David Maher / SPORTSFILE)

Bernard Dunne with former WBO super middleweight champion Steve Collins at the Burlington Hotel, Dublin (Brendan Moran / SPORTSFILE)

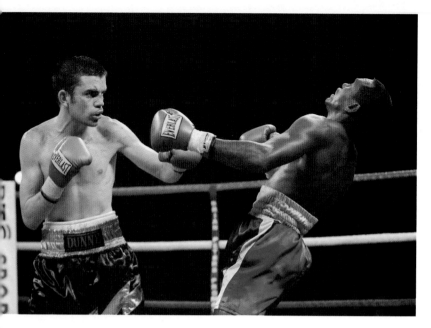

Super bantamweight bout, Bernard Dunne v. Felix Machado, Breaffy House Hotel, Mayo, on 2 April 2008 (Paul Mohan / SPORTSFILE)

Bernard Dunne, right, and his trainer Harry Hawkins preparing for Dunne's title defence against Poonsawat Kratingdaenggym (Oliver McVeigh / SPORTSFILE)

Bernard Dunne exchanges punches with Poonsawat Kratingdaenggym during the second round of their WBA world super bantamweight title fight at the O2, Dublin, on 26 September 2009 (Stephen McCarthy / SPORTSFILE)

Bernard Dunne is given a count from referee Jean Louis Legland during the third round of his title fight with Poonsawat Kratingdaenggym (David Maher / SPORTSFILE)

Dunne could excel and take the title took faith on behalf of the press and, indeed, the bookmakers. However, Dunne was priming himself for probably the most important thirty-six minutes of his life. Harry Hawkins, Dunne and Peters had learned a lot from Kiko Martinez in the space of eighty-six seconds – and Ricardo Cordoba would soon realise just how much Team Dunne had taken out of that setback. There would be no complacency this time in the ring.

Speaking to the *Irish Times* in the run-up to the fight, Dunne explained that his team was leaving nothing to chance in respect of his preparations: 'I want to say after this fight that I've given myself every possible opportunity going in there. I don't want to be sitting here in two weeks' time saying I should have done this or that. I have had great sparring, indeed William Gonzalez has fought Cordoba. Both my partners are contenders themselves. They're not here to tip around to earn a few quid. They're here to work hard and to work *me* hard. William is a tall southpaw, a good mover. He's good at talking as well, and he's telling us what he thought he should have done better and what he thinks we should do. On my loss to Martinez, he believes it was part tactical and a lot mental. Still nothing is being left to chance.

'Technically I think I'm as good as anybody. But maybe I'll have to mix it up with Cordoba. And is he going to be this guy I expect when we get into the ring? One thing we've definitely learned from the Kiko fight is to make sure we're focused. This guy may come out and say this kid starts slow, let's get out and get into him. We've got to be ready for that. Mix it up, mix it up.'

When Dunne referred to the prospect of 'mixing it' with Cordoba, he was being realistic. What happened in the ring on the night in question was exactly how Dunne had called it; however, the performance to which he treated the Irish public has gone into the sporting annals as sheer brilliance.

13

THE FIGHT: BERNARD DUNNE
V. RICARDO CORDOBA

'O ye of little faith'

Brian Peters, at the post-fight press conference

For boxing fans, what occurred on 21 March 2009 in
Dublin's O2 Arena was quite simply a thing of beauty,
and a joy forever. When sport can create moments of
simple patriotic pleasure and mix it with pure theatre, it
is a delight to behold. For Ireland, that day provided not
one, but two memorable highs. In the late afternoon, the
last-gasp drama of the country's grand-slam triumph in
Cardiff set up perfectly Dunne's crack at glory later that
evening. The euphoria of Ireland's victory created a feel-
good factor across the island, and the watching masses
were not to be denied a further episode of greatness. For
those fans of the Noble Art who wrote off Bernard
Dunne's chances after he had been defeated by Kiko

Martinez, the third Saturday in March would prove to be redemption day for the 'Dublin Dynamo'.

The usual razzmatazz was in evidence in the O2 Arena as the great and the good of Irish society packed the venue to cheer on their hero. It was true to say that a vast majority of fans came that evening in hope rather than expectation, such was the task ahead of Dunne. However, with the news of the rugby team's win in Cardiff still causing a stir, the luck of the Irish could always lend a hand to Dunne. Brian Peters had left no stone unturned as he went about providing the Irish boxing public with a show that was unparalleled in its variety and drama. Within the arena, an elevated walkway had been constructed to add to the drama of Dunne's entrance; with puppets of Bono, The Edge, Larry Mullan and Adam Clayton doing the rounds, it was going to be a dramatic night.

The Dubs were in fine voice as the 'Olé! Olé, Olé, Olé!'s began early. The mood was exuberant, with Ireland's victory in the rugby setting the tone for the evening. The anticipation rose as the undercard progressed. In the main supporting bout, Andy Lee was to endure a tough ten-round encounter against Alex Sibos, but came through in the end on a 99–91 verdict. Despite the final result, the Limerick man suffered a cut above his right eye during the first round that was a cause for concern in his corner. In the sixth, he dropped the German, who gamely fought on, but by taking all but one of the rounds, Lee was a comfortable winner, and his performance was warmly received. The eye-opening performance of the night came in the form of the exhibition bout between world champion Katie Taylor and the American champion Caroline Barry. The crowd were impressed with the style and standard of the women's boxing. Taylor hit the front in the opening round and controlled the bout for the whole four rounds, to win convincingly. In the commentary box, Dave 'Boy' McAuley, who had previously been sceptical about women's boxing, was won over by Taylor's display. Irish wins came also from the Cavan boxer Andy Murray, who took the European Union lightweight title, defeating Daniel Rasilla on points. Meanwhile, Paddy Barnes easily won his own exhibition bout, while crowd favourite Jim Rock and Michael Kelly both won too, to make it a great night for the Irish. Dunne's moment arrived.

The dry ice, 'The Irish Rover' and the anthem all came and went in a blur. After the drama of the build-up, the moment of truth arrived as the bell sounded. The fight began in a crescendo of noise, with the taller Cordoba using his long jab to great effect to keep Dunne at bay. Soon the Dubliner began to make his mark with a couple of neat left hooks and combinations that shook Cordoba as he momentarily lost his composure. By the third, Cordoba recovered and took the fight to the challenger, boxing with renewed composure. Soon, Dunne reacted, and in the last half-minute of the round he came at Cordoba with vigour, planting a neat left hook to the champion's chin that had Cordoba on the canvas – and the crowd on their feet. The referee began the count as Dunne sensed that Cordoba was there for the taking, but with only twelve seconds until the bell, Dunne had no time to capitalise on his advantage. After the first three rounds, Dunne, despite what the critics thought, was holding his own with the champion; the expectation in the arena was growing. In the corner between rounds, Harry Hawkins exuded great calmness as he tended to Dunne; the fight was there for the taking. By the fourth, the complexion of the fight changed when Dunne's head opened up after a clash of heads. Regardless, Dunne threw some excellent left hooks, but the champion began to show some neat touches as he regained the upper hand. The crowd started to rally behind Dunne as it became evident that the Dubliner was going to have to fight tooth and nail to see off the craft and skill of Cordoba.

However, for all the good work of Dunne, the fifth round was almost disastrous for him. The round began with an accidental Cordoba slip and, despite the premature roars of the crowd, the champion began to gain the upper hand. As 9,037 fans of Dunne watched on helplessly, Cordoba opened up and, just one minute into the round, Dunne was knocked to the canvas for the first time. The signs were ominous; the undoubted boxing skills of the champion were coming to the fore, and Dunne was beginning to look somewhat dishevelled. After the count, Dunne tried to mix it with the champion but soon found himself on the end of another fast combination that sent him to the canvas for a second time. The battered and bloodied Dubliner seemed to be almost finished.

The crowd roared encouragement and the round ended with Dunne hanging on for dear life on the ropes as Cordoba went for broke. The champion fired at least sixteen clean shots that landed on Dunne; it was a vicious onslaught. At this stage, nobody would have argued with the referee if he had called a halt to the proceedings. He hesitated, and Dunne was saved by the bell. It had been a massive round for the champion and it seemed that Bernard's title hopes were almost at an end. There was plenty of work to do in Dunne's corner; it seemed that the fight was slipping away from the challenger.

For Dunne, composure was the name of the game as the bell sounded for the sixth round. Keeping the champion at a distance was vital, and Dunne threw his own combinations as his confidence returned. He survived the sixth and in the seventh began to reassert himself in the contest. It seemed that Cordoba's best shots had been absorbed by Dunne and the fight was still in the melting pot. As the eighth began, Dunne looked refreshed, and matched the champion blow for blow. Cordoba knew that, if the fight went the distance, he could be in trouble, as Dunne seemed to be growing in confidence and showing extraordinary fitness and durability. The champion came forward to try and take the fight to the Dubliner, but Dunne was fighting the bout of his life, in front of a crowd whose expectations were growing by the minute. In the tenth, Cordoba was dominant, and forced Dunne to display his skill at counterpunching. Cordoba again launched a flurry of body shots, pinning Dunne to the ropes, as the round ended. Yet the Irishman refused to yield to the onslaught as the fans roared encouragement. The bell sounded; Dunne was going nowhere, and Cordoba knew it. Far away from his native Panama, he was alone in an arena where the noise was deafening. Dunne was not going to give up easily: he had waited all his life for the chance to fight for a world title. The tide was turning.

By the eleventh, both men were practically out on their feet. The fight had entered the category of boxing classic and, as every minute passed, it was getting even better. Punches, uppercuts, jabs and hooks continued to be thrown at a unbelievable pace as the fight went one way and then the other. With a minute left in the round, it was Dunne who produced the punch that sent the champion to the floor for the second time. The crowd were ecstatic, but the champion was back on his feet quickly and, after the count, the order to 'box on' was given. Dunne was straight in, and soon Cordoba was on the canvas again. The clock showed forty-five seconds to go in the round. Dunne was just seconds away from glory, and Cordoba was out on his feet.

The referee thought about stopping the fight, but then thought again. Accuracy, power, skill, belief and stamina had got Dunne to the threshold of the world title, and he could almost taste the glory. Cordoba was a beaten man: the crowd sensed it, his corner sensed it, but

that he had made a full recovery, but the manner in which he had left the arena inevitably had an impact on Dunne's victory. The referee was coming in for some well-deserved criticism for the manner in which he had let the champion continue when it had been obvious that he was finished after the first knockdown of the last round. Dunne was enjoying his time in the packed ring as he received the belt and basked in the glory of the crowd. Almost sixty-one years to the day after Rinty Monaghan had claimed the country's first world crown in Belfast's King's Hall, Ireland had a new champion. Dunne had scaled the heights, defeated his demons and proved that he was the best in the world. The fans eventually left the arena and the partying continued into the small hours.

The reality for Bernard Dunne was that the only way he was going to win the contest as it entered the eleventh round was by a knockout. Whatever was said in the corner at the end of the tenth round obviously worked its magic. It was a truly epic end to a fight in which Dunne had been trailing – and which he would have lost if it had gone to a points decision. As *Fightnews.com* was to report: 'Dunne's Irish heart was just unstoppable on this night. He fought back and the war continued, both men giving no quarter. At the start of the eleventh round, Cordoba was ahead on the scorecards 95–92, 96–91, 97–90, and the title seemed headed back to Panama. However, the champion was exhausted and Dunne came out like a predator, sensing that he needed a knockout. Dunne battered Cordoba, floored him three times and made Ireland proud. An incredible turnabout.'

Afterwards, Dunne was to miss the post-fight press conference as dehydration set in. Not surprisingly, the gargantuan effort needed to sustain the fight for so long had drained every last ounce of energy from his body. As usual, Dunne's face showed the scars of battle all too prominently. He was exhausted and seemed distant as he made his way from the arena. Dunne was a true champion and, after changing, made his way to the Beaumont Hospital, where he stayed at Cordoba's bedside until the next morning. Boxing is a sport where triumph and tragedy can sometimes go hand in hand; Bernard Dunne knew that the fine line between these emotions had almost been crossed. The following day, as the reality of being world champion set in, Dunne said of Cordoba: 'I had a chat with him. He was good; they're just keeping him in for observation, a precautionary measure. I felt it was right to go in and see him because he put up a hell of a fight.'

Within the Brian Peters camp, it was a case of complete satisfaction. He had taken the gamble of going for the title fight and had worked his magic to pull off one of the greatest shows in Irish sporting history. Bernard Dunne had paid Peters back in kind for his faith in him. After taking the criticism on the chin for far too long, Peters relished the post-fight press conference, where, with great pride, he told the assembled hacks: 'Tonight was the biggest financial gamble of my life. There were a lot of naysayers out there. All I can say is "O ye of little faith".'

The following day, the great and the good of Irish society were jumping over themselves to congratulate the newly crowned super-bantamweight champion of the world. President Mary McAleese led the tributes by saying that Dunne had 'showed courage, skill and determination in winning like a true champion'. She added that the victory had been 'a wonderful occasion for him and his family, and one in which all of us can share'. The Minister for Sport, Martin Cullen, TD, congratulated Dunne too: 'I would like to congratulate Bernard Dunne, who, after a remarkable challenge, successfully captured the WBA World Super-Bantamweight title. It was a sensational performance by the young Dubliner. With determination, power and stamina he boxed his way to a memorable victory. Bernard Dunne's personal success in Dublin in front of thousands of supporters was the culmination of a wonderful day in Irish sport.'

The leader of the opposition, Fine Gael's Enda Kenny, despite getting former champion Barry McGuigan's weight division incorrect, congratulated Dunne and said it was wonderful for Ireland to win back the super-bantamweight world title after twenty-four years, when it had been held by McGuigan. 'Every credit is due to him, his family and the team which helped him to prepare for this incredible fight,' he said. Soon Bernard began his rounds of the television and radio studios. He told RTÉ's Marian Finucane that he 'couldn't wait to see the fight on TV as it was a great fight to be involved in . . . it was a long fight, it was a hard fight, it was one of those fights that takes a lot out of you.'

The good times rolled for Dunne. The pictures of the fight and the post-bout euphoria would soon become legendary. The nine thousand spectators present that night will, in all probability, end up as ninety thousand within a decade, such is the 'I was there' appeal of the evening. All was well, and Ireland basked in the aftermath of a spectacular weekend of sport. Within days, an old friend weighed into Dunne's life in an audacious attempt to steal the Dubliner's limelight. Wayne McCullough sent an open letter to Bernard challenging him to put his belt on the line against him in an all-Irish box-off. It was, for the thirty-nine-year-old McCullough, a case of mission impossible. Despite McCullough's heroic status within the Dunne camp, the offer was predictably declined by Brian Peters, who consigned McCullough to the past tense: 'Wayne's a good friend and he's been a great servant to Irish boxing as well as a great world champion. However, he hasn't won a fight since 2004, so he really would need to put together a few good wins, including a win over a ranked contender, before it could be considered a viable fight.

'At the moment Bernard is taking a well-earned break and enjoying his success. It was an incredible fight and an incredible night and we're certainly not short of options now. As I said after the fight, the world is his oyster and there are all kinds of avenues open to us now. It's a case of taking our time and working out what the best move is but we certainly won't rush into anything. Obviously now that Bernard's become a world champion he's in a very strong position. The dream fight would be a big Las Vegas showdown with Israel Vazquez. He's currently sidelined with a few long-term injuries but is considered one of the best pound-for-pound fighters in the sport.

'It's a clash Bernard would relish as he sparred with Vazquez day in, day out as a young pro when he was out in Los Angeles, and I think those sparring sessions proved to a lot of people that Bernard had what it takes to reach the very top of the sport. You also have guys like Celestino Caballero who is eager to fight Bernard. He [Caballero] says he'd be willing to come to Ireland, so right now there are a lot of options to consider, including the possibility of a voluntary defence for Bernard at home in Dublin.'

Whoever he faces, or whatever he does during the rest of his career, the events in the O2 Arena on 21 March 2009 tilted the world on its axis ever so slightly in favour of Bernard Dunne. As Brian Peters pointed out, the world became his oyster that spring evening. Dunne became the super-bantamweight champion of the world, and nobody will ever take that away from him. Being a world boxing champion – like being an Olympic boxing champion – stays with you for life. A person's reputation is measured in such achievements. In a generation, Dunne will still be a champion, and introduced to everyone as such. It is said that nothing succeeds like success and, in the case of Bernard Dunne, this is certainly true. In fact, some people are born to be champions, and Bernard Dunne has been truly blessed.

14

THE ECSTASY AND THE AGONY

'A man's errors are his portals of discovery.'

James Joyce

As Bernard Dunne would soon discover, the novelty of being world champion doesn't last long. The problem about being at the top of your sport is that everyone wants to knock you off your pedestal. The good times can only last for so long until it's time to face the reality of defending your title. For Bernard Dunne, the glory of his victory over Ricardo Cordoba may have been the pinnacle of his career to date, but his legacy was still a work in progress. The doubters and begrudgers, many of whom had been silenced by the bravery that Dunne had shown to defeat Cordoba, could still claim that the Dubliner had 'touched lucky' to take the title. To prove he was a worthy champion, Dunne would have to silence his critics yet again, with a successful defence against a top-class opponent.

As the damp Irish spring turned into yet another damp Irish summer in 2009, the speculation mounted as to who would be named as the first challenger for Dunne's title. Talk of a 'unification bout' with the IBF and WBO champions was muted, while the name of Israel Vazquez came to the fore as a potential challenger. In reality, Brian Peters knew that he could no longer afford himself the luxury of picking and choosing Dunne's opponents; from now on, it would be total class all the way. The WBA would be dictating matters thenceforth, but Peters was keen to secure a voluntary defence before the mandatory challenger – Poonsawat Kratingdaenggym of Thailand – had to be faced. Speaking to the boxing website *eastsideboxing.com* in June 2009, Peters explained the predicament in which Dunne found himself:

'It's early days obviously, and it looks like Poonsawat could be our mandatory challenger. So I might have to fly over to Venezuela to meet with the WBA to see exactly what the situation is with that, because my preference would be Vazquez. We'll have to see whether we can get in a voluntary and then give him [Poonsawat] the mandatory shot. The other possibility is that we go straight for a unification bout with IBF champion Celestino Caballero or WBO champ Juan Manuel López.'

Eventually, in late August, the news broke that Dunne would defend his title on 26 September against the number one challenger, the aforementioned Poonsawat Kratingdaenggym of Thailand. Poonsawat was a former kick-boxing champion; his record in the ring showed that he was a truly class act. He had fought thirty-nine times and had lost just once – the only time he had fought outside his native Thailand. He was ranked as the number one super-bantamweight by the WBA and had been waiting a full eighteen months for his chance to fight for the title. In reality, this was not the fight Brian Peters or Dunne either wanted or needed. However, natural justice dictated that Poonsawat could not be denied his chance; eventually, his patience would have to be rewarded with a date in Dublin with the champion. In considering the ability of his opponent, Dunne knew that he would be facing a dangerous fighter:

'He's got fantastic ability, is a great puncher and he's been waiting for eighteen months for somebody to box him, so I'm willing to give him a chance. Let's see what he can do. I've been training now I think for three months or so, and it's been a tough training camp. It's been hard, especially with not having a face to focus on, but now it's 100 percent guaranteed it's Poonsawat, and now I have something to focus on.'

Ominously for Dunne, Poonsawat possessed a powerful punching ability and was referred to as Thailand's very own Manny Pacquiao. (Pacquiao, like Poonsawat, had a squat style and a devastating punch; he had used both to brutal effect in May 2009, when he dispatched England's Ricky Hatton to retain his world light-welterweight crown.) Of his thirty-seven victories, twenty-seven had come by way of knockout; Bernard Dunne was facing the biggest threat to his career since the Kiko

Martinez fight in 2007. In addition, Poonsawat, like Dunne, had a victory over Ricardo Cordoba to his name, while his only defeat had come in Germany in 2006, when the then WBA bantamweight champion, Wladimir Sidorenko, shaded a narrow decision. As with Cordoba, the fact that Dunne's opponent seemed vulnerable outside his native country was seen as a positive. Yet he had never been floored. For Poonsawat, however, he believed that fate and ability would make him world champion.

'I've been waiting for this chance for a very long time but I've kept busy and I am very determined to finally get what I deserve,' Poonsawat said. 'I believe that I will knock Dunne out inside seven rounds. I watched that fight and both Dunne and Cordoba are good boxers but I'm not sure that Cordoba was in the best of shape for that fight . . . . Clearly Dunne has a great fighting heart but I don't see him as a very skilled boxer. He proved against Cordoba that he has a big heart and maybe he is a big puncher too, but we will see what happens next month.'

Brian Peters, however, remained upbeat and was confident that Dunne had become an even better fighter since the Cordoba fight. 'Poonsawat has been waiting for a shot at the title for over eighteen months now, so he's a very determined man. He says he has no fear coming to Dublin to take on Bernard, but let's not forget that Ricardo Cordoba said exactly the same thing. Bernard's performance against Cordoba was absolutely sensational. The heart, conditioning, skill and power he demonstrated on the night proved once and for all that he belongs up there with the very best, and the scary thing is that I believe there is still more to come from Bernard. His strength and conditioning coach, Mike McGurn, believes that Bernard can improve three-fold even on that performance, so that's a scary prospect for any fighter, even one as good as Poonsawat.'

The scene was thus set for the showdown. Irish boxing began to brace itself for Bernard Dunne's next night of drama. The sport was on the crest of a wave as the 9,500 tickets for the bout went on sale: Bernard was without doubt the most popular sportsman in the country. However, the sport of boxing in Ireland was to suffer a crippling body blow on 14 September 2009, when news broke of the death of one of its most talented sons.

The passing of Olympic middleweight bronze medallist Darren Sutherland deeply shocked Irish sport and would cast a dark shadow over the bill at the O2 Arena. When the St Saviour's boxer returned from Beijing in 2008, it seemed that the world was his oyster. Offers poured in for the talented Dubliner to turn professional; in October that year he signed terms with London-based promoter Frank Maloney. On 18 December 2008, Sutherland began his paid career with a knockout of Georgi Iliev in Dublin. Three further victories followed over the following seven months, as Sutherland based himself in an apartment in Bromley, London. He was certainly a star on the rise in the paid ranks. His death came as a devastating blow to everyone who knew him and followed his career; the lonely reality of professional boxing was put in perspective.

The tragic news of Sutherland's death cast a long shadow over the build-up to the fight. Bernard Dunne had been affected by the passing of a friend but had to remain focused in the days leading up to his title defence. Poonsawat arrived in Dublin to a tumultuous welcome from the city's indigenous Thai population. He meant business and believed that his devout Buddhist faith, which provided him with an inner calmness, would inspire him to victory. The Thai possesses angelic features that belied the destructive potential in his fists. He was small and muscular, and, most notably, confident about his ability to defeat Dunne. Speaking through his interpreter, he outlined his game plan for the fight; worryingly for Dunne, the Thai was hoping to win with punching power. It seemed that for Dunne, it would be a battle of character and endurance yet again.

'I have to knock him out and not rely on the scorecard and I have to finish it before the twelfth round,' Poonsawat remarked, showing an inner steeliness that belied his choirboy looks. 'I'm happy to be here to fight Bernard Dunne, but it's kind of sad that Bernard has to lose his title in the first defence.'

In reality, the spectre of the Kiko Martinez defeat had haunted Dunne since he had lost his European belt to the Spaniard in 2007. While Dunne had shipped some cracking punches from Cordoba in their world-title battle, the fact was that Poonsawat was a harder puncher than the Panamanian. Indeed, the Thai boxer possessed a bustling style that was not unlike Martinez's. For Dunne, the top priority was to avoid a brawl with Poonsawat; how this was to be achieved over twelve rounds was a poser in itself, however. The game plan for the Dubliner would be to keep the fight at distance, jab and move, and, most importantly, avoid a 'dust-up'. The bottom line was that Poonsawat was probably the most skilful, toughest and certainly the most dangerous opponent that Dunne would ever face. The bottom line was that he would need to match – or better – his performance against Cordoba.

The media circus continued throughout the week as the fight drew close. As usual, the pundits made predictions as the bookmakers called the odds, with Dunne installed as the slight favourite. The home crowd was seen as a factor in his favour, while Poonsawat's lack of experience outside Thailand was viewed as crucial. The appointed time arrived for the weigh-in at the Old Jury's Hotel in Ballsbridge. It was a confident and supremely fit Dunne who mounted the scale, to come in a full half-pound under the eight-stone-ten-pounds limit. Ten weeks at the Holy Trinity Gymnasium in west Belfast had left the Dubliner in peak physical shape. And with that, he was off to continue his preparations. Next up on the scales was Poonsawat, who came in right on the weight limit; bang on the money. And with that, he clasped his hands, bowed to the press and supporters, and disappeared from sight. Since he had arrived in Dublin, the

Thai boxer had maintained a dignified persona; he seemed to possess an inner confidence and belief in his own ability. Friday passed, and the appointed hour drew near for both Dunne and Poonsawat. History dictated that an Irish world champion had never lost a title on home soil. From Rinty Monaghan and John Caldwell to Barry McGuigan and Steve Collins, the omens looked good for Bernard Dunne. However, boxing history also dictates that omens sometimes count for little when the first bell has sounded.

From the early morning of Saturday, 26 September, the O2 Arena was alive with familiar sounds as the preparations for the contest neared an end. The noise of hammers and drills was interspersed with the testing of public-address systems, while a plethora of officials, with the obligatory clipboards, ran through their various checks. Bit by bit, the ingredients for the showdown were falling into place. By early evening, the patrons were beginning to fill the various watering holes close to the O2 to discuss the intricacies of Dunne's defence, while in the arena the undercard commenced.

By 9.30 PM, the arena was alive as the build-up continued. RTÉ began its build-up with Mick Dowling, Andy Lee and Jim Rock giving their considered analysis in the studio. When the appointed hour arrived, the drama began: Poonsawat entered the cauldron – to a less-than-enthusiastic Dublin welcome. In keeping with his devout faith, he paused and prayed long and hard before entering the ring. It was evident that he was completely focused; he would not be distracted by the crowd's huge support for Dunne. It was, perhaps, first blood to Poonsawat.

The crowd now awaited their own gladiator. The 'Olé! Olé, Olé, Olé' chorus began in earnest as the great and the good of Irish society prepared for the main event. Six months had passed since the last instalment of the Bernard Dunne story, and the crowd were hungry and baying for more. Eventually, the tried-and-tested classical music 'O Fortuna' filled the arena, and the dry ice filled the air. After a dramatic, light-filled crescendo, and then a pregnant pause, the champion appeared as the first bars of 'The Irish Rover' belted out from the speaker system. Dunne was back, and the crowd loved it. He began his familiar walk to the ring, looking pensive and determined, but this time he had the WBA belt in his possession: it was a statement of intent. With both fighters in the ring, the formalities of anthems, introductions, eyeballing and final words of inspiration began. This was the moment of truth for both boxers, and the time for talking was over. There would be no turning back.

In the studio, RTÉ's Dara Moloney sat beside Dunne's gleaming belt as each of the three pundits gave their view that Dunne would win. Mick Dowling, however, having represented Ireland at two Olympics, and as the holder of a record nine Irish senior titles, was being realistic. He knew that Dunne would win only if he kept the fight at a distance, and added that Poonsawat 'was not here for the trip'. Dowling, it seemed, knew that whether Dunne could keep the fight at a distance was the big 'if'. It was now over to Jimmy Magee and Dave 'Boy' McAuley, as an expectant nation settled down to watch the drama unfold.

There were only three men left in the ring as the bell rang to signal the start of the contest. The early exchanges were fast, with Dunne showing the slicker touches, keeping his opponent at a distance. The crowd reacted with a roar each time Dunne landed a punch on Poonsawat, while the Thai fighter kept calm and composed. Dunne had a three-inch height advantage over his opponent, who moved with intent after the Dubliner. The bell rang to signal the end of the first round – which Dunne had taken with ease. However, in the corner he was being told emphatically that he had to fight the next eleven rounds in exactly the same manner as he had approached the first: don't let him get inside you, and don't get involved in a brawl. Afterwards, Poonsawat described the opening round: 'In the first I was just trying to get close and see his style and see how hard he could hit. But after that, I knew that he could not hurt me and I knew that I could win.'

In the second, Dunne began to feel the power of Poonsawat as the Thai opened up with his clunking fists. The Dubliner was definitely on the back foot, as the former kick-boxer pressed home his advantage. Things were beginning to look ominous for Dunne. The third round began, and it was evident that Dunne was troubled by his opponent. He was looking around, trying to buy time as the pressure on him built. It was Dunne against the hungry fighter, and the 9,500 fans packed into the O2 Arena could only look on helplessly.

With scarcely a minute gone in the third round, the challenger caught Dunne with a powerful left hook to the head, and put him on the canvas. It was a case of déjà vu: the ghost of Kiko Martinez had appeared in the guise of Poonsawat. Silence descended upon the arena – pierced only by the distant cheers of the Thai's supporters. Dunne had been in this position before, but never against someone of the calibre of Poonsawat. He got up, looked at the floor, then at the referee, who told the fighters to box on. Dunne had beaten the count but the round had still to reach its halfway point. The crowd roared him on, but Dunne could feel the title slipping from his grasp as Poonsawat came at him with gusto. Soon, another left hook caught Dunne, and he was down. The French referee, Jean Louis Legland, began the count as Dunne took his time to get back up. It was almost a fait accompli: the Dubliner's reign had only seconds left to run. Then the *coup de grace* came, again with the left hook, as the towel was thrown into the ring from Dunne's corner. It was over: three knockdowns in one round automatically ends a fight, according to the WBA. Dunne was prostrate in the ring, and the medics took up their positions beside the defeated champion.

It was a truly crushing defeat for Dunne, who was soon on his feet, although he was obviously dazed by the three hooks which had ended the fight. The arena resembled a wake: the Thai – 'The Silent Assassin' – had taken the title in the most emphatic fashion. Bernard Dunne's six-month reign was over. Again, as in the aftermath of the Martinez fight, Dunne bravely faced up to his obligations and spoke to RTÉ's Marty Morrissey in the ring in an interview that was relayed to the departing crowd. Dunne was somewhat lost for words. He apologised to his fans for having been lured into a fight with his opponent – a mistake for which he had paid the ultimate price. 'It's going to take a long time to get over this, but I will get over it,' he added, as a distressed Pamela watched on from the ringside.

The pundits soon analysed the fight, and they were not kind to Bernard Dunne. He had been a marvellous and worthy world champion but had been up against an opponent who was far superior to him. Irish Olympic gold medallist – and personal friend of Dunne – Michael Carruth suggested that it was time for Dunne to retire after the manner of the defeat. *Irish News* journalist Eamonn O'Hara captured the moment of defeat perfectly in his considered report: 'When fire is played with, expect to get severely burned. Bernard Dunne, amazingly, ignored the warning signs. The finality of Poonsawat's ruthlessly executed finish, and the brutal beating he handed out, brought a hushed silence to the Arena before the auditorium respectfully applauded the Thai's stunning performance.'

In the *Belfast Telegraph*, David Kelly, who had followed Dunne's career for more than a decade, had this to say on the Dubliner's defeat: 'Just as two years ago when losing the European title to Kiko Martinez, whose stature Poonsawat resembled, Dunne was cut down in clinical fashion. He was a pitiful sight as his legs resembled [those of] a newly born foal and his eyes were lost in a sea of distress. The fists were still pumping out blows but the engine was packing up as Poonsawat sent him to the canvas on three occasions.'

However, the most telling piece came from Tom Humphries in the *Irish Times*, who in an article entitled 'Thanks Bernard, now look after yourself' asked if the demise of Dunne in the ring was a bit too akin to the 'pornography of violence'. On Dunne's future in the boxing ring, Humphries said: 'I hope he ends it now. There is no easy road back for a man crowding thirty, and the memories he has left the Irish sporting public should be complicated by no more bad nights. Bernard wants to be a firefighter when the gloves are put away, and we would worry about him less were he running into burning buildings for a living rather than running into the likes of Poonsawat Kratingdaenggym.'

The whys and wherefores, and the ifs, buts and maybes of the defeat were chewed over for many days as Dunne took stock of his defeat. The speculation continued as the gravity of the defeat sank in. Brian Peters felt that a move to featherweight remained 'certainly a possibility' for Dunne, adding that he felt that Dunne would return to the ring at some stage. For Team Dunne, there would be no quick decision on Bernard's future:

Peters said that it would take time to explore all the possibilities:

'Obviously we're all very disappointed right now, but once the dust settles we'll look at our options and see what direction we go from here. There are no excuses, Bernard was beaten by a great, great fighter last night and I'm sure that Poonsawat will enjoy a long and successful reign, and we wish him all the very best for the future.'

The year 2009, which saw Bernard Dunne claim the world crown on that never-to-be-forgotten night in March, ended in tears and pain as the Dubliner's dream was well and truly shattered. On 26 September, Irish sports fans did not celebrate late into the night, as they had in March; instead, they contemplated, as reality bit hard. There was to be no second fairy-tale ending for Dunne: his ultimate flaw – the fact that his style is of no use against a boxer with a powerful punch – had been exposed yet again.

Regardless of what Bernard Dunne does in the future, nobody will ever take away from him the glory of the victory over Cordoba. And perhaps, after a period of reflection, Dunne will realise that the sights and sounds of that heroic night will only diminish should be take further punishment within a boxing ring. The key to a successful career in professional boxing is knowing when to retire unhurt, and with your pride intact; perhaps that time is close at hand for Bernard Dunne.

Appendix A

Bernard Dunne's Professional Record

Born: 6 February 1980, Neilstown, County Dublin
Fought 30, Won 28, Lost 2

2001

19 December: bt Rodrigo Ortiz, Oroville, California, TKO 2

2002

2 August: bt Christian Cabrera, Mashantucket, Connecticut, TKO 2

2003

3 January: bt Simon Ramirez, Norman, Oklahoma, KO 1
7 February: bt Eric Trujillo, Las Vegas, TKO 1
1 March: bt Oscar Villa, Tustin, California, PTS 4
25 April: bt Oscar Rosales, Norman, Oklahoma, TKO 1

6 June: bt Terrell Hargrove, Uncasville, Connecticut, KO 1

3 July: bt Mario Lacey, Chester, West Virginia, KO 1

3 October: bt Julio Cesar Oyuela, Albuquerque, New Mexico, TKO 2

7 November: bt Alejandro Cruz, Tucson, Arizona, PTS 6

2004

12 March: bt Evangelio Perez, San Jose, California, PTS 6

27 March: bt Angelo Luis Torres, Tustin, California, PTS 8

2 July: bt Pedro Mora, Pala, California, PTS 6

19 August: bt Adrian Valdez, Maplewood, Minnesota, PTS 10

2005

19 February: bt Jim Betts, National Stadium, Dublin, TKO 5

May 14: bt Yuri Voronin, National Stadium, Dublin, PTS 10

14 October: bt Sean Hughes, National Stadium, Dublin, TKO 2 (IBC super bantamweight title)

10 December: bt Marian Leondraliu, Leipzig, Germany, TKO 2

2006

28 January: bt Noel Wilders, National Stadium, Dublin, TKO 6

3 April: bt Sergio Carlos Santillan, Rivarolo Canvaese, Italy, PTS 8

3 June: bt David Martinez, National Stadium, Dublin, TKO 8

11 November: bt Esham Pickering, Point Depot, Dublin, PTS 12 (EBU super bantamweight title)

2007

25 March: bt Yersin Jailauov, The Point, Dublin, TKO 3 (EBU super bantamweight title)

23 June: bt Reidar Walstad, The Point, Dublin, PTS 12 (EBU super bantamweight title)

12 August: lost Kiko Martinez, The Point, Dublin, TKO 1 (EBU super bantamweight title)

2008

12 April: bt Felix Machado, Castlebar, Ireland, PTS 10

12 July: bt Damian David Marchiano, Dublin, Ireland, W 10

15 November: bt Cristian Faccio, Dublin, Ireland, W 7

2009

21 March: bt Ricardo Cordoba, O2 Arena, Dublin, TKO 11 (WBA super bantamweight title)

26 September: lost Poonsawat Kratingdaenggym, O2 Arena, Dublin, TKO 3 (WBA super bantamweight title)

APPENDIX B

BARRY MCGUIGAN

Prior to 1978, the market town of Clones in County Monaghan was best known as the home of the annual Ulster Gaelic football final. Each July, the town came to a virtual standstill as thousands of spectators poured in from across the province to witness the best players in Ulster football slug it for the Anglo-Celt Cup at the picturesque St Tiernach's Park. On such occasions, the shops, bars and restaurants in and around the town's central diamond did a roaring trade. The second Sunday in July was indeed the highlight of the year in Clones.

However, from 1978 until the late 1980s, Gaelic football was eclipsed as the number one sport in Clones by boxing, as a local lad named Barry McGuigan began to put the town on the world map. His career became the talking point in streets, shops and bars as he established his credentials as one of the greatest boxers produced by this island. For the town that would become known as 'Barrytown', a legend was in the making.

Finbar 'Barry' McGuigan, the son of Pat and Katie, was born into a family of five boys and three girls on 28 February 1961. Prior to assuming the mantle of fame, another member of the McGuigan family had already come to international prominence when Barry was a mere seven years old. For one night in April 1968, Clones was the talk of Monaghan, Ireland and Europe, as Barry's father represented Ireland on the stage at the Royal Albert Hall in the 1968 Eurovision Song Contest.

Pat McGuigan (or 'McGeegan', as he was to become known, thanks to a misspelling of his name on a promotional poster) finished in a creditable third place at the contest with his rendition of 'Chance of a Lifetime' – and Ireland was truly delighted. McGuigan Senior was placed behind the evergreen Cliff Richard, who had been hot favourite with the catchy 'Congratulations', while the contest was won by the truly memorable 'La La La' by the Spanish entrant, Massiel. In a dress rehearsal for the celebrations which Clones would host two decades hence, Pat McGuigan's return to the town on 8 April 1968 was a night to remember.

For a decade, though, there was not much more excitement in Clones. In the 1970s, the Troubles in the North cut the town's hinterland of County Fermanagh off as roads were cratered and blocked. Clones seemed to become just another 'border town'. But it was a border town with a difference: Pat McGuigan's son was beginning to learn his ring-craft. Boxing was in Barry McGuigan's blood from an early age. After an initial grounding in the sport in the nearby club in Wattlebridge, he soon settled at the Smithboro Boxing Club, approximately five miles from Clones. Under the keen eye of trainer Frank Mulligan, McGuigan progressed rapidly through the ranks and, by 1976, had claimed his first Irish junior title, defeating Martin Brereton. In February 1978, Barry McGuigan came of age when he won the Ulster senior bantamweight crown by beating Enniskillen's Kenny Bruce at the Ulster Hall.

McGuigan says that his victory in the Ulster Senior Championships accelerated his career and led to many memorable times in a period of uncertainty across the North. McGuigan gained his first green vest when he represented his country in an under-19 international in Drogheda in the spring of 1978. However, his amateur career soon suffered a setback when he was not picked to represent Ireland in the European Junior Championships, which were held in Dublin that year.

'I lost out to a guy called Hugh Holmes, whom I had beaten in the Irish championships, for the bantamweight choice in those Games, and it really cut me up badly,' he said. 'I was hurt inside and felt really hard done by, and when Holmes went on to claim a silver medal in Dublin, it was worse, as I felt that I could have claimed the gold if I had been picked.'

While the 1978 European championships were a disappointment for McGuigan, the anomalies of Ireland's North-South divide provided him with a chance to shine on a bigger stage. In August of that year, the eleventh Commonwealth Games were held in Edmonton in the

Canadian province of Alberta. The Northern Ireland side that went to those Games consisted of the cream of Ulster's champions; the Clones boy was on his way to fame.

'It was a fabulous experience from start to finish and I'll never forget the Games, for the spirit within the team was marvellous,' he said. 'We were under the guidance of Gerry Storey and we stayed in the Stella Maris hostel in Belfast prior to the Games to get the collective training done. I'll not say that it was the most exclusive of surroundings, but we were very well looked after. The team gelled together. It was my first experience of collective training. We worked out in Newcastle, County Down, and I remember that we did sprints and boxed three times a day, which left me so fit. Once in Edmonton, we stayed beside the Northern Ireland bowlers and we became really friendly, as they could not do enough for us. The thing about major Games is that everyone is looking out for everyone else in their team, and as someone progresses, the goodwill and expectations grow, which leads to a great spirit. The boxers that year were a really exceptional bunch and the rest of the Irish team were fantastic in the way they encouraged us all the way.'

The boxing squad that represented Northern Ireland that year was indeed an exceptional collection of fighters. Barry McGuigan took gold in the welterweight division, as did Ballymena's Gerry Hamill in the lightweight class. Kenny Beattie claimed a silver medal, while Hugh Russell from the New Lodge area in Belfast claimed a bronze.

McGuigan's progress through the bantamweight competition was fairly straightforward. In the final, he was to meet the dangerous and well-built Papua New Guinea fighter Tumat Sugolik. Sugolik had powered his way through the competition. As McGuigan explained, his trainer, Gerry Storey, had made sure that McGuigan had not seen the muscular fighter, and he was surprised when his opponent climbed into the ring:

'I remember I was getting changed for the fight and I noticed this guy in the corner and could not believe his build; I thought he was a couple of divisions above bantamweight and felt that I was lucky not to have had to fight him. When I climbed into the ring and saw that this person I had seen in the changing room was to be my opponent, I had no time to let it sink in and just had to get on with it. I suppose it was reverse psychology by Gerry Storey not to let me see this guy who had been knocking out everyone in front of him, and it worked in my favour in the end.'

McGuigan outfought the Papua New Guinea fighter to get the decision, but recalls that he found himself on the end of one of his haymakers. The thought of this punch still makes him wince to this day. 'He caught me during the fight and I thought honestly that my head was going to come off my shoulders,' McGuigan recalled. 'He was a crude and heavy-handed fighter and he packed some punch. It was the hardest one I had taken in my career to date.'

Adorned with the gold medal, McGuigan's tears on

the podium in Edmonton as the strains of 'The Derry Air' echoed through the arena caught the imagination of the people back home. The image of an inconsolable seventeen-year-old first put the name and the face of the Clones lad into the hearts of the Irish public. Barry is convinced that his tears were an expression of the frustration he had felt over not being picked for the European Games earlier in the year.

The 1978 Commonwealth Games produced a plethora of exceptional fighters. McGuigan recalls one encounter with a future world champion with pride: 'Mike McCallum, who became a world champion in 1984 by defeating Sean Mannion to win the world junior middleweight title, was representing Jamaica and he had beaten our own Kenny Beattie to claim gold at lightweight,' he said. 'I remember meeting him at a get-together after the finals and I will never forget what he said to me. He looked at me and said "I'll see you at the top son." . . . In the featherweight class, the great Azumah Nelson won the gold, so it was quite a Games in boxing terms.'

The next step in McGuigan's progress was the Olympic Games, which were scheduled to be held in Moscow in 1980. Unfortunately, in the run-up to the Games, he broke his hand in a contest; he was in a race against time to be ready. With the hand on the mend, Barry was duly picked to wear the green vest in the featherweight division. In the first round, McGuigan was afforded a bye, and in his first outing he defeated Issack

Mabushi of Tanzania after the referee stopped the contest in the third round. However, his moment of victory proved pyrrhic.

'I remember after the decision was announced I was going over to the corner to see the coaches and I heard the BBC commentator Harry Carpenter say that I seemed to be having no problems with my injured hand. I knew that there was still a problem, as in my sparring I was having difficulty with my timing and accuracy due to the injury since, I knew, it had not healed completely. Just as I heard Harry mention that my hand seemed OK, I was advising Gerry Storey that I was in pain and having problems with it. In those days, the solution was to freeze the hand with an injection of anaesthetic that would see you through your bout without pain.'

The medicine was duly administered for Barry's next bout against the Zambian Winfred Kabunda, but the damage had been done, in terms of McGuigan's frame of mind, and he lost the bout on points.

'The fight with Kabunda was one of only three fights I lost as a senior amateur fighter, and I was very disappointed to be out. In his next bout, the Zambian was in turn defeated by the eventual gold medal winner, Rudi Fink from East Germany, so it was a bitter experience. I was only left to think what could have been, but we all fell in to support Hugh Russell and he ended up with a bronze, so that provided me and the team with some consolation.'

With the Olympic dream now gone, McGuigan took

the plunge into the paid ranks and in 1981 signed terms with the County Tyrone-born, Belfast-based bookmaker, Barney Eastwood. Belfast – and Northern Ireland – was still going through its nightmare, with politics on the street being dictated by events concerning the hunger strikes in the Maze Prison. It was a huge gamble at the time for anyone to contemplate the return of professional boxing to the city, but McGuigan's class was worth the risk. Based in the Eastwood Gym in Castle Street, McGuigan came under the watchful eye of former professional fighter Eddie Shaw.

McGuigan's first outing as a professional came on a cold May night in 1981 at Dublin's Dalymount Park. That bill marked the beginning of the end of Charlie Nash's career, while Selvin Bell was no match for the body-punching of McGuigan, and was duly stopped within two rounds. A win over Gary Lucas in four rounds in London was followed by McGuigan's first setback, when he lost a hotly disputed decision in Brighton to Peter Eubank, the elder brother of Chris. Undeterred, the McGuigan machine rolled into Belfast a month later; the Ulster Hall was to witness a boxing renaissance.

Victories over Jean-Marc Renard in September, and Terry Pizarro in October, set up the yearned-for rematch with Eubank. On 8 December 1981, a packed Ulster Hall saw McGuigan take his revenge, stopping Eubank in the eighth and final round.

A series of victories followed, but the tragic death of the Nigerian boxer Young Ali after a bout in London with McGuigan in June 1982 saw the Clones man plunged into grief and despair. After much soul-searching, he decided to carry on with his career. A victory against Jimmy Duncan in October 1982 set up a final eliminator for the British title against the hard-hitting, and previously undefeated, Hastings-based Paul Huggins. Huggins was duly stopped in the fifth round at the Ulster Hall, and the following April Vernon Penprase offered little opposition, being stopped in the second round at the Ulster Hall. At twenty-two, McGuigan was now British champion, and the road to world domination was becoming clearer.

The inevitable progression towards a crack at a world title continued for the 'Clones Cyclone', as he was now nicknamed. The King's Hall in Belfast was resurrected as a boxing venue for McGuigan's European title fight with Valerio Nati in November 1983. A crowd of seven thousand witnessed him stop the Italian in the sixth round. The class of his opponents was increasing as he closed in on the title held by the legendary Eusebio Pedroza.

During 1984, a series of encounters convinced the Belfast public that McGuigan was ready for the highest stage: four victories at a packed King's Hall, one at the Royal Albert Hall, and a successful defence of his British and European titles against Clyde Ruan.

Juan Laporte was a classy Puerto Rican fighter who fought out of New York City. He had gone punch for punch with Eusebio Pedroza in a world title bout, only to lose on points. For his endeavours, the World Boxing

Council matched Laporte against the Colombian Mario Miranda for the vacant title at Madison Square Garden. When Miranda failed to come out for the eleventh round, Laporte won the bout and became world champion. He went on to defend his title twice, winning both on points, before losing out to the legendary Wilfredo Gómez. Laporte was certainly the toughest opponent McGuigan had faced.

The two men met in Belfast on 23 February 1985. It turned out to be McGuigan's hardest battle and he took a vicious punch from Laporte half-way into the fight that almost stopped him in his tracks. Barry composed himself to win on points after ten bruising rounds to prove conclusively that he was able to mix it with the best and, most importantly, take a punch.

Belfast and Ireland was engulfed in frenzy as arrangements were finalised for the fight with the reigning WBA champion, Eusebio Pedroza, at Loftus Road in London on Saturday, 8 June 1985. The fight attracted a crowd of over 25,000 to the ground and was beamed live across Britain and Ireland to record audiences. From the rendition of 'Danny Boy' by Pat McGuigan, to the sight of a leprechaun waltzing through the ring before the fight, the event was surreal for all who witnessed it. In the seventh round, McGuigan caught Pedroza with a sweet right hand and over the champion went. Twice more McGuigan had Pedroza sprawling in the ring, but all the skill and guile acquired over seven years as champion kept him in the fight. Fifteen fraught rounds were fought out in their intensity and as McGuigan was declared the champion, the party began in London. That party carried on across the Irish Sea and engulfed Ireland for a number of days. The scenes in Belfast and Dublin as McGuigan was welcomed home were unsurpassed. Seventeen years after Pat McGuigan had brought Clones to a standstill through his singing ability, a far bigger reception awaited his feted son.

The fact is that in Barry McGuigan's professional career, those nights in June 1985 were to be the pinnacle of his achievements. The old adage goes that, once you reach the top, there is only one way things can go. Defeat, acrimony, comebacks and court cases all followed in the wake of the glory. However, in those nights in the 1980s, all was well; and maybe that is the way it should be remembered.

Barry McGuigan was in the correct place at the correct time in an era when Northern Ireland was hungry for hope and happiness. He provided that in abundance. That is only half the story, though. The 'Clones Cyclone' learned his trade through dedication and a will to succeed. Nobody can take away his achievements nor question the ability that has established him as one of the foremost pundits in modern boxing. On the wall of his gym, as he was learning his trade, a crudely painted slogan told McGuigan what was required to succeed in both boxing and life. It read: 'Work hard, think fast and you will last!'

Wise words that have proved to be true for Barry McGuigan.

Appendix C

Wayne McCullough

There lives in Belfast, in a part of the Upper Crumlin Road known locally as the 'Turn of the Road', a man in his eighties by the name of Al Gibson. He is a proud man steeped in Ulster boxing history and wisdom, having enjoyed a fine record as a professional in bygone days. Al Gibson is a walking encyclopaedia of Ulster and Irish boxing. He speaks with passion of the sport he loves. As he rhymes off the names of the fighters whom he has known over the decades, he speaks in hushed tones as he describes their evident greatness.

When he talks of the recent past, he gets to the name of one Wayne McCullough and pauses. Then, with a sharp intake of breath, Al Gibson's eyes widen, as he takes off his glasses and says with a knowing smile: 'Now, Wayne McCullough, there's a proud boy and a half! He has it all and proved it on the very highest stages, and when I think of that fight in Japan. What more can I say, son? Absolute Genius!'

Wise words from a gentleman of Ulster boxing, who lives not two miles from the street where Wayne McCullough was born on 7 July 1970. Percy Street, between Belfast's Shankill and Falls Roads, was in the eye of the political storm that had erupted in the city that previous August. Indeed, the week of Wayne's birth coincided with a pivotal event of the Troubles known as the Lower Falls Curfew. Community relations in the city were at a low and worsened considerably over the succeeding years. The McCullough family, which consisted of three brothers and four sisters, soon relocated to the Highfield Estate at the top of the Shankill Road. Highfield was situated perfectly for young boxers as the Albert Foundry Club stood off the nearby West Circular Road. At the age of seven, Wayne found himself at the club under the watchful eye of trainer Harry Robinson.

'My two brothers Noel and Alan were boxing, and I couldn't wait to join them,' he recalled. 'I was about seven when I started and Harry Robinson guided me in the early days when I must have had over a hundred fights by the age of twelve. Davy Larmour, who went on to be a British bantamweight champion, was at the club as a professional and he was always someone to look up to.'

At the age of eleven, McCullough passed his eleven plus examination and left Springhill Primary to join the local secondary school, Cairnmartin. His career in the ring continued unabated, with his sole aim to turn professional at the earliest opportunity. In 1986, the Highfield boxer won his first Ulster senior boxing crown, with a convincing win over the vastly more experienced PJ O'Halloran. An international debut against Scotland followed in which he stopped his opponent, Donald Glass.

By 1988 Wayne McCullough had acquired Ulster and Irish titles in the light-flyweight division. At eighteen years of age, he was on his way to Seoul as the youngest representative of Ireland's Olympic squad. It had been traditional for the youngest member of the squad to be asked to carry the Irish Tricolour at the opening ceremony, but, for a lad from the greater Shankill area, this honour was not as straightforward as it seemed.

Boxing is an all-Ireland sport and always has been. The border is irrelevant in the sport, as it is in rugby, cricket and hockey. However, the sight of a lad from the loyalist Highfield Estate parading the flag of the Irish Republic became a political football in the North.

'The whole flag issue was blown out of proportion, as I was doing it for sporting reasons and nothing else,' said Wayne. 'Pat McCrory, our coach, came to me and asked if I would carry the flag, which to be truthful put me in bit of a position. I said that I would do it for sporting reasons alone, and entering that stadium is one of the most unforgettable moments of my life.'

In his opening bout, McCullough was paired with the lanky Ugandan fighter, Fred Mutuweta. The Belfast fighter was awarded a unanimous decision after he floored the African in the second round. In his next fight, Wayne was drawn against the Canadian Scotty Olsen, the reigning Commonwealth champion. After receiving two standing counts during the bout, McCullough's Olympic dream was at an end. On his return, the Shankill Road threw a party for its favourite son: nobody mentioned the carrying of the flag.

After Seoul, McCullough was persuaded to bide his time before entering the paid ranks. A trip to the 1990 Commonwealth Games in Auckland, New Zealand, saw him victorious in the flyweight division, where he defeated Nokuthula Tshabangu of Zimbabwe for the gold medal. More memorable than McCullough's win was the medal ceremony, which did not go as smoothly as the organisers had anticipated.

As Wayne was standing on the podium, with his gold medal around his neck, the recording of 'Danny Boy' jammed in the tape player to a deafening silence in the arena. However, cometh the hour, cometh the man, and into the ring jumped Northern Ireland expatriate and Games official Bob Gibson. With microphone in hand, he sang the traditional air unaccompanied to steal the show and create a long-lasting friendship with Wayne. Indeed, soon after, Gibson was the special guest of honour at Belfast's Europa Hotel as Wayne fought at a Golden Gloves evening, where he repeated his feat to an appreciative crowd.

Soon after he returned from the Games, Wayne was to meet his soul mate and future wife Cheryl Rennie. In November 1990, McCullough travelled to the World Cup in Bombay where he battled his way to claim a bronze medal, again at the expense of his Seoul opponent Fred

Mutuweta. McCullough duly followed this achievement with a trip to the 1991 World Championships in Sydney. There, he blazed a trail through his division and was unlucky to lose in the quarterfinals against the eventual silver medallist, Enrique Carrion from Cuba.

At the Barcelona Olympics in 1992, McCullough's experience and pedigree made him favourite to lift a medal. He travelled with high expectations as Ireland's bantamweight representative in August that year. The swimmer Michelle Smith carried the flag on that occasion, and it was to prove to be a memorable Games for Irish boxing.

As the Irish boxing team were eliminated one by one, both McCullough and team captain, Michael Carruth, found themselves fighting for gold medals on finals' morning. McCullough in his opening bout had seen off – yes, you've guessed it – the Ugandan Fred Mutuweta on a comfortable 28–7 scoreline. He followed that victory with a win over the Iranian Ahmad Ghanim and was then drawn to meet Mohammed Sabo of Nigeria.

McCullough negotiated that fight with relative ease, and had assured himself of at least a bronze medal. In his semifinal bout, he was drawn to meet the Korean Li Gwang-Sik and nine minutes of pugilistic warfare ensued. McCullough's all-action style and volume of punches won the day on a scoreline of 21–16 points. Both he and Carruth were now into the finals. Ireland, north and south, waited with bated breath.

Wayne's fight with the classy Cuban, Joel Casamayor,

proved to be a painful experience, in more ways than one. A typically slow start by McCullough saw him trail 6–1 after the first round. In the second, a scoring jab to Wayne's face by the Cuban caused him serious discomfort.

'He hit me with the jab and I felt the pain in my cheekbone,' recalled Wayne. 'My face was numb and in reality I should not have fought on.'

Trailing by 10–2 at the end of the second, McCullough bravely went out for the last and out-boxed the Cuban convincingly. Despite a storming comeback he was defeated on a scoreline of 14–8.

'I was determined to finish the fight and by the end there was blood coming out of the corner of my eye. I had lost after giving it my best shot but the damage to my face was a huge price to pay as I didn't fight again for a year.'

An hour after his defeat, Wayne watched Michael Carruth make history. 'I remember that I saw Michael's fight on the television in the medical room in the arena as I was taking a drugs test; it was a truly special moment.'

With an Olympic silver medal to add to his other amateur accolades, Wayne McCullough had gone as far as he could in unpaid boxing. Unfortunately, for him, the glory days of Barry McGuigan had passed and the professional ranks in Belfast were going through a lull in the early 1990s. His only option was to leave his native city to pursue a professional career in the United States under the management of an American television executive called Matt Tinley. A move to Las Vegas followed for

Wayne and Cheryl, and his rise through the world bantamweight rankings was swift.

By the turn of 1995, under the legendary trainer Eddie Futch, McCullough had gone fifteen fights undefeated. A victory over Geronimo Cardoz in March that year secured him a crack in Japan at the reigning World Boxing Championship holder Yasuei Yakushiji. Only the keenest and closest accompanied the Belfast boy, and to the serenade of Bob Gibson singing 'Danny Boy', he left his Tokyo hotel for his ultimate moment. Dedication and training in the freezing Albert Foundry gym during the 1970s had finally brought McCullough to his ultimate hour. By the time he returned to the hotel, he would be the champion of the world.

At the end of twelve fabulous rounds, the two boxers, bruised and battered, came to the centre of the ring to await their fate. To Wayne, the Japanese announcer went through the formalities which made sense to all but one hundred of the ten thousand crowd. After an age, the announcer paused and roared out his rough translation of the name McCullough. The boy from the Shankill had just become the champion of the world. Tears, joy and pandemonium erupted in the ring as the dream became reality.

In many ways, it can be argued that the fact that McCullough went to Yakushiji's hometown to fight for and win the world title elevated what he achieved. On the other side of the world, in an intimidating arena, he was to fight the greatest twelve rounds that any Irish fighter had ever fought. One thinks of John Caldwell fighting

Éder Jofre in Sao Paulo in 1962 as the only comparable experience for an Irish fighter. Caldwell lost that night; in 1995, McCullough won.

In December 1995, Wayne McCullough defended his title at the King's Hall, the shrine of Belfast boxing. That night in front of a packed hall he stopped the Dane, Johnny Bredahl, in the seventh round. The homecoming as champion was complete.

McCullough defended his title again in March 1996 with a points victory over Jose Luis Bueno, before vacating the belt and moving up a weight to challenge Daniel Zaragoza for the world super-bantamweight crown. That fight in January 1997 was a tremendous battle. The bout went to a split decision and McCullough lost narrowly. It was his first defeat and he was devastated by the experience. That fight left McCullough with a broken jaw, minus two wisdom teeth. However, even darker days lay ahead.

In 1998, McCullough fought Naseem Hamed in Atlantic City for the IBO world featherweight title. A points defeat for the Belfast man was a considerable setback in his attempt to climb the world rankings. In October 1999 he fought Erik Morales for the super-bantamweight crown, losing again on points.

In October 2000, a fight was arranged in Belfast for McCullough. Prior to the fight he attended the Royal Victoria Hospital for his yearly brain-scan, which was obligatory under the British Boxing Board's rules. Two days before the fight, he was told that a cyst had been discovered on his brain. In essence, a punch to the head could end his life.

'That was the lowest point in my life,' recalled Wayne. 'Cheryl and I could only sit about the house and I became very depressed. But I am a fighter and it was a case of trying to establish the extent of the problem and making sure that it was addressed.'

In Las Vegas, the Nevada Boxing Commission suggested that McCullough consult with a specialist based at the Department of Neurosurgery at University of California in Los Angeles. After an examination, he was advised that the cyst was not actually on his brain, but in the narrow space between the brain and the skull, and this should not impact on McCullough's career. Accordingly, the Nevada Commission relicensed McCullough and, in 2002, he once again entered the ring, to face Alvin Brown, who he stopped in two rounds. Eventually the British Board relented and McCullough was authorised to fight in Britain. Wayne McCullough's last fight took place in July 2005, when he fought Oscar Larios for the second time and lost on points again.

Living in and training fighters in Las Vegas has allowed Wayne McCullough to maintain a presence in the sport he loves. After all his trials and tribulations, it is not surprising that he had found great faith in God.

'Sure I miss Belfast but it was boxing that took me here and we are settled in Las Vegas. Cheryl took me to her church in Belfast soon after we started dating, and my faith is something that has grown with me ever since.

When you enter a ring, you really need someone to look after you and for me that someone is God. I am good friends with George Foreman, who is a preacher, and he has been a great influence on me.'

Wayne's career in boxing continues unabated. He has scaled the heights in both amateur and professional ranks. His memories of his early days are vivid; even though Las Vegas is a long way from the Belfast he grew up in. 'Belfast was a hard city to grow up in, especially if you were from the generation that I came from,' he said. 'I was lucky as the fact is that boxing bridged all the religious stuff, and we trained and fought anywhere in the city. Now I have a number of Mexican fighters in my gym and they are so like the Belfast fighters. For what they lack in skill, they more than make up for in guts and determination. These boys have a survival instinct: that same instinct has helped Belfast and Ireland produce so many good fighters. However, I think that Michael Carruth was a true great, if not the greatest amateur to come out of Ireland. Having won a gold medal at the Olympics, he did what no other boxer from Ireland did. I read a recent article where he stated that he thought me going to Japan to win the belt was the best achievement of any Irish boxer. The feeling's mutual, as his achievement in Barcelona was immense.'

Wayne McCullough, his wife Cheryl and daughter Wynona live a contented life in Las Vegas. We have not heard the last of him in boxing terms. He has been an exemplary and brave fighter who represented the best attributes of the sport.

APPENDIX D

STEVE COLLINS

Where were you on the night of Saturday, 18 May 1995? If you had a passing interest in the world of boxing, you were most likely glued to the television for the first instalment of Steve Collins's clash with the strutting arrogance that was Chris Eubank. The town of Mill Street in County Cork, with its magnificent Green Glens Arena packed to the rafters, was to witness the highest of drama as the showman met the hardman in a never-to-be-forgotten battle. Drama, 'codology' and sheer brutality was to ensue as Collins dethroned the then-reigning World Boxing Organisation super middleweight champion with a sublime display of aggression. Eubank may have been self-styled as 'Simply the Best' but it was Collins who took that mantle and engraved his name forever on the list of Irish boxing greats.

Steve Collins was born in Cabra in Dublin on 21 July 1964. The sport of boxing was in his blood from an early age as his uncle, Jack O'Rourke, won three Irish senior titles during the sixties, while his father, Pascal, was also a very accomplished fighter in his day. Another uncle, Terry Collins, had a notable victory over the East End gangster Reggie Kray to his name, so it was natural that Steve Collins would enter the ring at some stage. In 1986, as an amateur, Steve emulated his uncle Jack by winning the Irish senior middleweight crown but, due to the weak Irish economy, he left Ireland to make a living in Boston. Collins took the well-worn route of most Irish immigrants to the States and made a living through a number of low-paid jobs to keep his family solvent.

While living in Massachusetts, Collins turned professional and joined the world-famous gym of the Petronelli brothers, who had in their ranks none other than Marvin Hagler, the then middleweight boxing champion of the world. Under various trainers, Steve's first paid fight saw him stop the comparative novice, Julio Mercado from Mexico, in the third round of their contest in October 1986. Six further victories followed within eighteen months and a fight with Sam Storey for the Irish middleweight title was set for Boston in March 1988. The previously undefeated Storey was dispatched on a unanimous decision after ten gruelling rounds. After five straight victories, Collins was matched with Kevin 'Killer' Watts, who at that stage was rated number five in the world, for the USBA middleweight crown. That fight in Atlantic City in 1989 saw Collins in classic slugging style and he took the title despite being dropped to the canvas in the eleventh round. Despite ploughing a lonely furrow in the United States, Collins was gaining valuable exposure on network television and quite a following in the Boston area.

A successful defence of his middleweight title led to a crack against the legendary Jamaican Mike McCallum in 1990 for his WBA middleweight title. While he had the 'home' advantage of a Boston venue, Collins went the distance only to lose his unbeaten record on a unanimous points decision. However, Collins had given the Jamaican such a battle that he expressed his reluctance to put his title on the line again against the 'Celtic Warrior'. In the aftermath of the defeat to McCallum, Collins found himself back making a living behind a bar in Boston. Undeterred, the Dubliner continued to make his mark and in August 1989 he knocked out Fermin Chirino in the sixth round of their bout at the Boston Sheraton hotel. After a further win in Boston against the tough Eddie Hall, Collins decided to move home and signed up with the Belfast gym of Barney Eastwood.

In April 1992, Collins secured a second crack at the then vacant WBA middleweight title when he was matched against Reggie 'Sweet' Johnson in a fight scheduled for East Rutherford, New Jersey. The title had been vacated when Mike McCallum had opted to fight James Toney for the IBF crown and with Collins ranked as number one contender and Johnson number two, a battle royale was anticipated. At the age of twenty-eight, Collins was at his peak and the fight with Johnson was a classic, with Collins considered unlucky to lose on a majority decision. 'The death of my father at the time of the fight was a low point in my life and affected me very deeply. The Johnson defeat was so devastating for me. I had a lot going on a personal level and it was hard to come to terms with it. I really had to dig deep to find the inspiration to continue my career after that.'

It was the second defeat of his career and his next outing was against the undoubted class of Sumbu Kalambay for the EBU championship in Kalambay's adopted home of Italy. A third defeat was recorded – again on a split decision – by the 'Celtic Warrior' in Italy. Soon after Collins split with the Eastwood stable by amicable agreement and signed up with the London-based Barry Hearne. Within a year, Collins had captured the WBA Penta-Continental middleweight title with a knockout over the South African Gerhard Botes at Earl's Court in London. Collins's star was rising in Britain and he was to capture the WBO middleweight crown a year later when he knocked out the champion, Chris Pyatt. Going into that bout, Collins was considered to be the underdog as the classy Pyatt was defending his title for the fourth time. However, Collins made no mistake in a display of controlled aggression to stop the champion in the fifth round.

At this time in Britain, Sky Sports was making its mark with its football and boxing coverage. The super-middleweight scene was flourishing with Chris Eubank, Michael Watson and Nigel Benn all setting the pace on the satellite channel during the decade. In 1990, the

Brighton-based Eubank defeated Nigel Benn by a knock-out in Birmingham to claim the world super middleweight crown and he went on to defend it twice against Michael Watson. The second fight with Watson ended in near tragedy after Eubank caught his challenger with an uppercut, causing an injury that ended Watson's career and left him with serious brain damage. Many observers felt that Eubank, who considered quitting the ring after the Watson fight, was a different fighter after that ill-fated clash. His reluctance in future bouts to go for a knockout became evident as his style changed to one of going the distance to grind out points victories.

Irish interest in the super middleweight scene was to occur initially in the shape of Belfast's Ray Close. As Irish and European Boxing Union champion, the Barney East-wood-managed Close had fought Eubank to a standstill in Glasgow in 1993 and came away with a draw. The scene was set for a rematch in the King's Hall in Belfast in May 1994, and a packed arena witnessed a bloodthirsty encounter that the champion shaded in a split verdict. The fight in Belfast did not resolve the matter and a third episode in the Close and Eubank affair was arranged for March 1995. Unfortunately, a routine brain scan on Close showed up some irregularities that forced the hand of the British Boxing Board of Control to ban the Belfast fighter. However, waiting in the wings for his chance was Steve Collins and the fight with Eubank was arranged for Mill Street in Cork on St Patrick's weekend 1995.

Irish sport in the 1990s threw up a number of

notable occasions in which, if not present, the general public can recall with absolute clarity where they where when the event took place. The famous David O'Leary penalty against Romania in the 1990 World Cup, together with Michael Carruth's triumph in the 1992 Olympic Games, were just two occasions of the decade that had the nation glued to the television; the Eubank v. Collins match was to be the third. With Sky Sports hyping the fight to the heavens, tickets for the clash at the nine-thousand-seater arena in rural Cork sold out within hours of going on sale.

Showmanship is one of the great traits of professional boxing and the then unbeaten Chris Eubank was the ultimate showman. His style outside the ring was ridiculed as he adopted the persona of the monocled country gentleman. Indeed, he had bought for himself the aristocratic title of Lord Brighton, such was his devotion to the class system. Collins was having none of it and went out to match the showman in the mind games. A few days prior to the clash, word seeped out that Collins had visited a number of hypnotherapists to help him with his preparations for Eubank. Collins let it be known that he had been 'programmed' to fire two punches for every one thrown by Eubank and the mind games had begun.

As the fighters entered the ring, the psychological war had been won by Collins. Sitting in his corner, listening obliviously to his Walkman, he displayed the greatest of indifference as Eubank began his flamboyant and melodramatic journey to the ring. To say that Eubank was affected deeply by the whole episode would be a correct assumption: the champion was spooked.

The fight began in whirlwind style with the undefeated Eubank posing and choosing his shots against the game Dubliner. Collins kept chasing the champion and had the arena in uproar as he gave Eubank a torrid time. By the tenth round, Eubank seemed to be slightly ahead on points when he threw caution to the wind and floored Collins with a right. Eubank was unable to finish his opponent and Collins stormed back.

With the capacity crowd now on their feet, Collins continued his onslaught and the sight of Eubank's trainer Ronnie Davies slapping his face in the corner at the end of the round to revive him told the tale. Collins chased and harried Eubank and exposed his showboating for what it was time and time again. The final bell went, the decision went to the judges and Collins was declared the winner. Eubank had lost his unbeaten record and Collins was now the star of Irish sport. In the rematch the following September, Collins was a comfortable winner. The unanimous verdict in Collins's favour led to Eubank quitting the sport and Collins then set his sights on defending the title.

'That was undoubtedly the highlight of my career,' said Steve. 'You cannot believe how intense things were between us and there was no love lost I can tell you. I got so much pleasure in that victory and it was sweet.'

Two further defences for Collins followed within nine

months. A win at the Point Depot over Cornelius Carr was followed by a knockout victory at Mill Street over Neville Brown. However, Nigel Benn was still a contender for a crack at Collins' title and the two were matched in July 1996 in Manchester. Collins won the fight when Benn retired on his stool at the start of the sixth round. A rematch was set for November but Benn, then aged thirty-two, was not the fighter he had once been and again retired in his corner after six rounds.

In February 1997, Collins retained his title when his fight with Fred Seillier was stopped due to cuts sustained by the challenger. At the Kelvin Hall in Glasgow in July, Collins, despite being down in the first round, stormed back to stop Craig Cummings in the third round of their bout. That was Collins's seventh successful defence of his title and he seemed to be untouchable in the division.

In Collins's next defence, he was matched with Joe Calzaghe, but the 'Celtic Warrior' was forced to withdraw at a late stage before the bout due to injury picked up in training. The WBO took severe action and stripped Collins of his title and he duly retired. In a parting shot, Collins claimed to have lost his motivation to step into the ring. He felt that his only viable option had been a unification bout against Roy Jones Jr, but this had been denied and a fight with Calzaghe would do nothing for him.

Two years later, Collins decided to come out of retirement to face Joe Calzaghe. The clash with Calzaghe was arranged for Cardiff on 5 June, but Collins blacked out during sparring with the British middleweight champion Howard Eastman and underwent a CAT scan. The doctors told Collins that a further blow to the head could result in his death. Collins had no option left and he retired from the ring for the second time. 'It was over and I just had to accept it. I had enjoyed my career and been lucky enough to work with Marvin Hagler, my all-time hero. He and Jake La Motta were the two men I always tried to emulate and my style was based on them.'

Although the glory years of the mid-1990s are remembered fondly, the probability was that Collins, Eubank and Benn were not at their peak when they formed their rivalries. The WBO title was a class below the WBA and WBC titles, yet it served its purpose and kept the British and Irish public enthralled. Steve Collins was an honest, strong contender, and proved to be an honest, strong champion.

Tough as nails, he once boasted that Readymix Concrete wanted to sponsor his chin. A showman, a fighter and without a doubt a hard man, Steve Collins caught the imagination and admiration of the British and Irish public. Today he remains a personality of note in Dublin and Ireland.

THEY SAID . . .

'I suppose you could say he has almost single-handedly brought professional boxing to a very, very high level here.' *MICK DOWLING*

'He'll be very downhearted for a few weeks because he feels he has let everyone down – his whole family, the whole nation. But there are opportunities still there because he's got great support.' *COACH HARRY HAWKINS*

'It is a tough time here for Irish people, Irish boxing people, especially with the passing of Darren [Sutherland]. I wanted it so badly this week just to give a little joy.' *BERNARD DUNNE*

'Obviously we're all very disappointed right now but once the dust settles we'll look at our options and see what direction we go from here. There are no excuses, Bernard was beaten by a great, great fighter last night and I'm sure that Poonsawat will enjoy a long and successful reign and we wish him all the very best for the future.' *PROMOTER BRIAN PETERS*

'I think he's done enough, but if he was to retire today he's had a great career and we'd all be immensely proud of him. If he's to bow out, bow out at the biggest stage, and that's a world title fight.' *OLYMPIC GOLD MEDALLIST MICHAEL CARRUTH*

'I'll be back. I've been down before and came back to win a world title. It will take a long time but I'll be back.' *BERNARD DUNNE*